PROTEST FROM THE RIGHT

Robert A. Rosenstone

Associate Professor of History
California Institute of Technology

GLENCOE PRESS
A Division of The Macmillan Company
Beverly Hills

For my parents —
who helped more than they know.

GLENCOE PRESS
A Division of The Macmillan Company
8701 Wilshire Boulevard
Beverly Hills, California 90211
Collier-Macmillan Canada, Ltd., Toronto, Canada

Library of Congress Catalog Card Number: 68-17296

First printing, 1968
Second printing, 1970

Preface

With the seventh decade of the century just over, it is already obvious that future historians will regard the 1960's as an era of protest. In the space of a few years, hundreds of groups — some of them minuscule, others with large memberships — have arisen and proclaimed in words and deeds an immense dissatisfaction with the state of American society. A good deal of this protest has come from traditional sources on the political left, and has concerned itself with such perennial questions as equal social, political and economic rights. Much more unusual is the fact that a great amount of protest has come from people calling themselves conservatives, people who are definitely on the right-hand side of the political spectrum. It is the purpose of this book to provide an introduction to the sources, nature and ideology of the many groups involved in this new protest from the right.

Like any complex phenomenon, right-wing protest can be approached in various ways, and this book will employ several different perspectives to give insight into it. Most important for understanding the right are original sources, documents written by its adherents, and a number of them are printed here. In truth, there is no quicker way to get the feeling and knowledge of what the right is about than to read the words of its leading spokesmen, and there is no better method than this for understanding the anguish and fear with which rightists view the changing American scene.

Here is the way this book will explore the problem. After an Introduction describing the rise of the phenomenon in the 1960's, Chapter One, through extensive quotation from original sources, gives a picture of the world as seen through the eyes of the right, showing how communism is believed to be the cause of all the ills besetting America. Chapter Two consists of longer selections by rightist leaders; here the emphasis is on getting the "feel" of their approach to the world, on understanding the emotional basis of their beliefs. Chapter Three includes magazine articles which describe how right-wing protesters carry their beliefs into action on the American scene, while Chapter Four presents negative reactions to the far right's activities by government officials and by various spokesmen for American conservatism. In Chapter Five, three scholars attempt to put the phenomenon into some sociological and historical perspective. Finally, the Suggested Readings will lead those who are interested to the best sources for a deeper study of the protest from the right.

Los Angeles, California   R.R.
October, 1970

(NOTE.—Throughout this book, the author–editor's footnotes are marked by symbols—*,†—and the original quoted notes by numerals.

(The capitalization of the word *communist* has been left as it was found in all reprinted materials, though the author prefers to capitalize it only where the Communist Party is specifically referred to.)

Contents

Introduction

Shortly after the inauguration of John F. Kennedy as President of the United States in January, 1961, the American press began to headline stories about an organization that few people had heard of before, even though it was more than two years old—the John Birch Society. Ostensibly dedicated to the ideal of "more responsibility and less government," the society seemed worthy of headlines partly because of its semi-secret nature and its monolithic structure (with all decisions being made by one man at the top), but especially because of the political views of its founder, leader and chief spokesman, Robert Welch, a retired candy manufacturer from Belmont, Massachusetts. Welch maintained that Kennedy's predecessor, Dwight D. Eisenhower, was a conscious, dedicated agent of the "Communist conspiracy" who had spent eight years in the White House leading the United States down the path to communism—it was this statement more than any other that made the John Birch Society as newsworthy as it was.

From the first, many people did not know what to make of Welch and the John Birch Society. While the American population has shared a kind of generalized anti-communism in recent years, few citizens were ready to believe, with Welch, that Eisenhower and his chief appointees, such as Secretary of State John Foster Dulles, were agents of the Kremlin, or that Presidents Truman and Roosevelt had willingly worked toward a communist takeover of the country, or that "democracy is a . . . perennial fraud." Few, also, were willing to agree that Earl Warren and the Supreme Court posed a greater threat to America than the armed forces of the Soviet Union, and almost nobody countenanced the John Birch Society tactics for combating communism, which Welch himself said were "mean and dirty." These tactics included copying the methods of the communists, organizing small cells of hard-core believers, setting up "front organizations" to dupe people into fellow-traveling with the John Birch Society, and harassing opponents in a wide variety of ways. At the beginning, most people tended to lump the John Birch Society together with the tiny "lunatic fringe" element in American politics.

When newspapers, magazines and government officials began to expose and denounce the John Birch Society in 1961, large numbers of letters to editors and Congressmen showed that, rather than being supported only by a handful of fanatics, Welch had many backers. Some of them deplored his charges about Eisenhower, but all were concerned over what they saw as the increasing communist influence in the United States. Before long it became evident that the John Birch Society was only one of a large number of organizations forming a significant group in American society, all sharing the feeling that the United States was losing the worldwide struggle against communism and that it was doing so largely because domestic communists and their friends had infiltrated every major institution of American life (including government, churches and schools) and were in the process of successfully subverting the country from within.

Political commentators and social scientists began to use a number of different terms to describe these anti-communist groups, including "radical right," "superpatriots," "ultras," "pseudo-conservatives" and "extremists." While what they are called may not be of absolute importance, the varying terminology shows that there has been some disagreement on the defining characteristics of these organizations. In this book, the reader will have the opportunity to hear their anti-communist voices, assess them in action and read analyses of their behavior; perhaps by the end he will be able to write his own definition. Meanwhile the groups together will be referred to as the *extreme* or *far right*. The word *right* is used in its traditional sense, referring to the conservative side of the political spectrum. *Extreme* and *far* are employed to modify *right* because these organizations do not simply want to conserve existing political and social institutions, but wish to turn the clock back to the institutions of an earlier age, at least pre—New Deal, perhaps even pre—twentieth century. They are relatively extreme in their analyses of problems facing the world and in their solutions for the problems, as will become apparent in the course of this book. Finally, they are extreme because they carry into the realm of politics a Manichaean view of the world: They see a rigid dichotomy between good and evil that ultimately forces them to reject the American political system as it has functioned since the beginning, with endless compromises between opposing points of view. To those on the extreme right there can be no compromise, for they believe that only evil men could wish to organize society in a manner different from their own ideals.*

Of course there is historical precedent for extremist ideas and even right-wing extremist organizations in the United States. They have always been with us. In the early days of the republic, extreme Federalists feared the Jeffersonians as men ready to overthrow the government in the name of the principles of the French Revolution, while in the mid—nineteenth century the Know-Nothings thrived on a Protestant fear of Catholicism and the Papacy.

---

*Extremists do sometimes take part in politics, but when they do they refuse compromise. A perfect example is the 1964 Republican convention in San Francisco, when rightist adherents who had helped Senator Barry Goldwater get the nomination refused to listen to compromise on any issues and harassed and booed moderate Republicans like Nelson Rockefeller.

INTRODUCTION

Moving into the twentieth century, one finds the violent Ku Klux Klan of the 1920's growing because people thought that Negroes, Jews, Catholics and foreigners in general were subverting and destroying the old America that they loved. Then came the thirties, rich in extreme political groupings; and while many were on the left, those on the right had large followings, too. Father Coughlin, openly anti-Semitic, claimed five million listeners to his radio broadcasts, while fringe groups like the Silver Shirts and the German-American Bund won some support for their pro-Nazi ideas.

Common among rightist groups, especially in the twentieth century, has been an anti-Negro, anti-Semitic, anti-foreign and often anti-Catholic ideology. Along with this, ever since the Russian Revolution, all extreme groups on the right have shared a militant anti-communism. For reasons that have never been satisfactorily explained, between the thirties and the late forties the feelings against Negroes, Jews, Catholics and foreigners seem to have receded from the panoply of acknowledged rightist beliefs. At least they were subsumed into an increasingly violent anti-communism. Thus Senator Joseph McCarthy, leader of a rightist crusade in the early fifties, was himself a Catholic, and two of his chief aides (Roy Cohn and David Schine) were Jews. Somehow these once-foreign elements had Americanized themselves, and they were able to join with older-stock Americans in a militant front against what they usually termed "atheistic communism." This is not to say that all anti-Semitic, anti-Catholic, anti-Negro "hate groups" disappeared from the American scene. But those that remain are truly part of a dwindling "lunatic fringe" and far less important in numbers, financial resources and influence than organizations like the John Birch Society, which concentrate solely on the menace of communism.

How many Americans are involved with far right organizations today there is no way of really knowing, though some estimates claim that five million people support them in one way or another. "Support," of course, may cover a wide variety of activities, from occasionally listening to a radio broadcast to subscribing to publications; from engaging in letter-writing campaigns to attending rallies. Appealing to this public are more than one thousand individual extreme right groups. Some consist of no more than one man, a mimeograph machine and a mailing list; but others, like Fred Schwarz's Christian Anti-Communism Crusade or the Reverend Billy James Hargis' Christian Crusade, have incomes of about a million dollars yearly and issue a wide variety of publications, tape-recorded lectures, and motion pictures, and sponsor radio and television broadcasts. Their appeal is evidently widespread; Hargis claims 130,000 subscribers to one of his publications, while commentator Dan Smoot reaches hundreds of thousands over his 110 radio and television outlets, and Clarence Manion, with over 300 radio and television stations carrying his weekly broadcasts, has an audience estimated at over a million. Though figures are far from certain, Birch Society membership today is thought to stand around the 100,000 mark. Other groups on the extreme right with a large following include the Conservative Society of America, run by Kent and Phoebe Courtney; Edgar Bundy's Church League of America; the Twentieth Century Reformation Hour, led by the Reverend Carl McIntire; and Myers G. Lowman's Circuit Riders.

To disseminate their message to the American public, the groups of the extreme right spend more than fourteen million dollars annually, with the amount having risen in recent years. How much more money than this they actually take in is not known. Of course some of their expenses are covered by small donations—the man who sends five dollars to the campaign to impeach Earl Warren, or pays eight dollars for a copy of Robert Welch's book *The Politician;* the woman who donates a small amount to Edgar C. Bundy to help root communists out of the Protestant ministry; the student who pays a few dollars to attend a Christian Anti-Communist school. But much of the support comes in large donations from tax-free foundations, from large businesses like Technicolor Corporation of America, Eversharp, Inc., the Schick Safety Razor Company, Dr. Ross Dog and Cat Food Company, and from wealthy individuals like Texas oilman H. L. Hunt.* All major groups of the extreme right have found their income steadily going up since 1960—there is little doubt that extremist groups are better financed today than they have ever been before in American history.

Of course, if the messages put out by the rightists fell on deaf ears, they would be of little importance, but since 1960 there has been little fear of this. Rather, large numbers of people have been willing to listen and to act upon the suggestions of the extremists. Commentators have argued over exactly who is doing the listening and acting, but most would now agree that there are more people involved than the "wealthy businessmen, retired military officers and little old ladies in tennis shoes" who were thought to characterize the Birch Society when it first appeared upon the national scene.† Though such types are certainly present, students of the subject have identified rightist adherents from all walks of life, including many professional men and white-collar workers with college educations. In spite of the fact that there are Jews and Catholics among the extremists, a high correlation can be found between support of the right and fundamentalist Protestantism. The reasons for this, and for the susceptibility of certain other social groups to extremist appeals, will be explored in various articles later in this book.

---

*A good summary of rightist finances can be found in Arnold Forster and Benjamin R. Epstein, *Danger on the Right* (New York: Random House, 1964), pp. 272–280.

†The quote was originally made by California Attorney General Stanley Mosk in "Report to Governor Edmund G. Brown on the John Birch Society," July, 1961, reprinted in *Congressional Record*, 87th Congress, Sess. I, p. 15869.

INTRODUCTION

The student investigating the subject of protest from the right should be cautioned at the outset that however far-fetched and even amusing their ideas may sometimes seem, as a socio-political movement the rightists are worthy of very serious consideration. One does not have to make comparisons (as some have done) between Adolph Hitler's *Mein Kampf* and Robert Welch's *Blue Book,* but neither should anyone ignore the fact that a number of powerful, militant groups of the twentieth century were originally considered no more than collections of crackpots. For when socio-economic conditions become disrupted, when war, depression or other calamities traumatize societies, when mass man—suffering from a crisis of faith—becomes unable to endure the burdens that an impersonal, corporate society places upon him, the will to believe that evil and mysterious forces are responsible for one's anxieties and troubles becomes overwhelming. In such a situation, the extremism of a fringe group could become the consensus of a nation.

Since the first edition of this book three years ago, the American scene has undergone drastic changes. As the Vietnam War has dragged on, militancy and violence have become more and more common in the United States, both in ghettos and on college campuses. Meanwhile a Republican administration has taken office, Earl Warren has retired from the Supreme Court and the issue of pollution has risen to national prominence.

Basically, such events have meant little to the Radical Right. At least its world view about the menace of communism has remained unchanged. Widespread demonstrations against the war and Black Power demands have only shown the Extreme Right the further progress of communism in America. With Warren out of the way, the drive for impeachment of the Supreme Court has focused increasingly on Justice William O. Douglas, supposed friend of Communists and pornographers. The unending war itself — with President Richard M. Nixon supporting it — has been seen as an attempt to drain America's resources, thus enabling Communists to more easily take over the country. Even the pollution issue has been suspect, and the well-publicized Earth Day (April 22, 1970) was believed a product of the Communist Conspiracy because it coincided with Lenin's 100th birthday. In short, while the issues may change, the Radical Right's beliefs remain constant. And with increasing social upheaval and dislocation, its appeal to those who want simple answers to complex problems remains a strong one.

The Insight Series
Studies in Contemporary Issues
from Glencoe Press

PROBLEMS OF AMERICAN FOREIGN POLICY
Martin B. Hickman

THE OPPENHEIMER AFFAIR:
a political play in three acts
Joseph Boskin and Fred Krinsky

THE POLITICS OF RELIGION IN AMERICA
Fred Krinsky

THE WELFARE STATE:
who is my brother's keeper?
Fred Krinsky and Joseph Boskin

OPPOSITION POLITICS:
the anti—new deal tradition
Joseph Boskin

IS AMERICAN DEMOCRACY EXPORTABLE?
Edward G. McGrath

PROTEST FROM THE RIGHT
Robert A. Rosenstone

DEMOCRACY AND COMPLEXITY:
who governs the governors?
Fred Krinsky

FERMENT IN LABOR
Jerome Wolf

AMERICAN ANTI-WAR MOVEMENTS
Joseph Conlin

THE POLITICS AND ANTI-POLITICS OF THE YOUNG
Michael Brown

URBAN RACIAL VIOLENCE IN THE TWENTIETH CENTURY
Joseph Boskin

POSTWAR AMERICA:
the search for identity
Donald G. Baker and Charles H. Sheldon

BLACK POWER:
the radical response to white America
Thomas Wagstaff

THE MEXICAN-AMERICANS:
an awakening minority
Manuel P. Servín

THE SUPREME COURT:
politicians in robes
Charles H. Sheldon

Series Editors: Fred Krinsky and Joseph Boskin

Chapter One

The Extreme Right Views the World

A helpful way of attempting to understand any social or political movement is to try to view the world through the eyes of its members. This is, of course, never easy to do. With the extreme right it seems especially difficult, for its perspective on the modern world is radically different from that of the majority of American citizens. The approach in this chapter will be to quote from a wide variety of documents and publications of the right in an effort to comprehend its world view. Though every person on the far right might not adhere to the exact letter of every quotation used, almost all would agree with the substance of the portrait that is painted. Here, then, is the extremist's universe, a world in which nothing happens by chance, in which all events have a definite cause, and a cause which the rightist can clearly discern.

The Menace of Communism

Central to the doctrine of the extreme right is the primacy of the communist menace. As one commentator pointed out, "It is not only an important thing in the world, it is the only thing."* And what is the nature of this menace?

> Communism is not a political party, nor a military organization, nor an ideological crusade, nor a rebirth of Russian imperialist ambitions, though it comprises and uses all of these parts and pretenses. Communism, in its un-mistakable present reality, is wholly a conspiracy, a gigantic conspiracy to enslave mankind; an increasingly successful conspiracy controlled by de-termined, cunning and utterly ruthless gangsters, willing to use any means to achieve its end. †

---

*Victor C. Ferkiss, "Political and Intellectual Origins of the American Radical, Right and Left," *The Annals*, CCCXLIV (November, 1962), 7.

†Robert Welch, *The Blue Book of the John Birch Society* (Belmont, Mass.: John Birch Society, 1961), pp. 30–31.

Naturally such a conspiracy must be combated, and the war against it is of universal importance, for it involves the ultimate principles by which men live. "This battle, the war-to-death struggle between freedom and communism, is actually a battle between Good and Evil, between the forces of Christ and of the Anti-Christ."* In this struggle, the time of Armageddon is close. Some on the right have actually given target dates for the takeover of the United States by communists; Fred Schwarz of the Christian Anti-Communism Crusade often mentions 1973. Others simply think it is too close for comfort.

> Communism is conquering the world! It is conquering the world in accordance with a definite blueprint and time schedule. The tentative date for the conquest of the United States is believed to be within the life expectancy of the majority of you in this room. †

> Unless we can reverse forces which now seem inexorable in their movement, you have only a few more years before the country in which you live will become four separate provinces in a world-wide Communist dominion ruled by police-state methods from the Kremlin. The map for their division and administration is already drawn. [Welch, p. 9.]

For those on the extreme right a good part of the world has already become communist-dominated, and their concern is largely with the United States. Though one might think that with its huge military establishment the United States would be secure from communist military ventures, the extremists find this view irrelevant.

> Many are falsely taking comfort in America's apparent armed might, but why should the Communists attempt to capture America by a two-ocean invasion, or by atomic warfare, when there are more than enough people inside the country willing to hand over the nation peacefully? Why should the great buildings and prosperity of America be reduced to rubble, when the Communists want these buildings and prosperity for themselves? America reduced to rubble would be of no value to the Communists.**

The key to this quotation, and to much of the extreme right's world-view, is the idea that "more than enough" Americans are willing to hand their country over to the communists. This process has begun already, and there is a consensus as to when such activities started.

> The soul of America began to be sold during the Franklin Roosevelt administrations. A price was placed on truth when this country recognized the anti-Christian regime of Red Russia. The process of deterioration and destruction of our free society under God became accelerated under the leadership

---

*"A Call to Action to Every Real American," leaflet (Tulsa, Okla.: Christian Crusade, n.d.).

†W. P. Strube, "Communism—A Conspiracy," (Houston, Texas, 1960), pp. 2–3.

**Billy James Hargis, *Communist America: Must it Be?* (Tulsa, Okla.: Christian Crusade, 1960), p. 17.

of Harvard eggheads. God gave us a chance in 1942–5 to be rid of both Nazism and Communism; instead our anti-Christian leaders chose to groom Communism for world leadership.

The providence of God gave us a respite under the administration of Eisenhower and Nixon, but it proved too little too late. The Kennedy administration began the final sell-out of this country to anti-Christian Communism.*

While all rightists would agree that the "selling out" of America began under FDR, large numbers would take issue with the idea of Eisenhower as a respite from this process. For many extremists the Eisenhower years made up the period when communism firmly fastened its grip on America. In running down a list of forty alleged communists high in Eisenhower's Administration, Robert Welch made the following comments:

> 1. Milton Eisenhower: . . . In my opinion the chances are very strong that Milton Eisenhower is actually Dwight Eisenhower's superior and boss within the Communist Party. For one thing he is obviously a great deal smarter. . . .
> 3. John Foster Dulles: . . . For many reasons and after a lot of study, I personally believe Dulles to be a Communist agent who has had one clearly defined role to play; namely, always to say the right things and always to do the wrong ones.
>
> . . . .
>
> 10. Allen W. Dulles: Head of the CIA . . . the most protected and untouchable supporter of Communism, next to Eisenhower himself, in Washington. . . .
> . . . I want to confess here it is my own conviction that Eisenhower's motivation is more ideological than opportunistic. Or, to put it bluntly, I personally think that he has been sympathetic to ultimate Communist aims . . . and consciously serving the Communist conspiracy, for all of his adult life. . . .
> But my firm belief that Dwight Eisenhower is a dedicated, conscious agent of the Communist conspiracy is based on an accumulation of detailed evidence so extensive and so palpable that it seems to me to put this conviction beyond any reasonable doubt. †

Not all on the right agree with Welch in his estimation of Eisenhower; even among members of the John Birch Society there have been some misgivings over this charge. But most think that communist agents have been infiltrated into high positions in all recent administrations.

> Within the past twenty-five years, Communists have been unusually successful in hiding their key men in the American Army, Navy, diplomatic corps, Treasury, Congress, and other control points of government. So great has been the infiltration that loyal, patriotic Christian American men and women still within the government are practically helpless, and those wanting inside, where they can be effective, cannot gain entry. [Hargis, p. 19.]

---

*Rev. Paul C. R. Peterson, newsletter of Awake America for Christ, (September, 1966).
†From Robert Welch, *The Politician;* quoted in *Congressional Record,* 87th Congress, Sess. I, pp. 5609–5611.

How far the communists have gone in control of the government is a matter of debate among extremists. Welch thinks the United States is 60 to 80 per cent communist-controlled. Others don't give percentages, but feel the situation is horrendous.

> For all intents and purposes, the government of these United States of America is now in the hands of the high command of Communist and liberal agitators whose professionally organized mobs have been set loose upon the American people. . . . The U.S. Constitution is in almost total de facto abeyance as these self-admitted revolutionaries, aided and abetted by agents and collaborators who have infiltrated every level of legislative, judicial and executive authority, strive for its final overthrow at the point of Federal bayonets.*

How have the communists seized so much control over the American government? They have not done so by proclaiming themselves party members and openly espousing Marxian doctrine, for the right believes such ideology in its unadulterated form to be anathema to the American people, the majority of whom are thought to be basically conservative. Obviously, the communists have had allies, people traveling the same road to collectivism but in a more roundabout way.

> America's totalitarian liberals do not, for the most part, admit to being socialists, because the general American public thinks it is opposed to socialism. For years, socialists participated in American elections openly but never received more than token support at the polls. Eventually convinced that Americans would not *wittingly* accept socialism, the socialists changed tactics. They infiltrated the major political parties and presented their old ideas under deceptive, new labels . . . they clamored for "government with a heart" . . . "social reform," a "welfare state."
>
> Modern liberals and socialists deny that there is any similarity between their program and communism; but the objective of communism . . . is identical with that of modern American liberals and socialists. . . .
>
> For the most part, American liberals have presented their socialist programs under false labels palatable to the people. . . .†

> Let me make it quite clear at this point that I am equating the welfare state and socialism—because they are one and the same. . . .
>
> Let me make it clear also that I am equating the welfare state, socialism *and* communism. While they may not be identical in every respect in the beginning, the end result of all of them is the same—the complete domination by the government of the affairs and lives of the people.**

Common Sense (June 1, 1965).

†*Dan Smoot Report*, (Nov. 11, 1963), 355–357.

**Thurman Sensing, "The Case Against the Welfare State" (Nashville, Tenn.: n.d.), 3.

Let the right understand, and fearlessly proclaim to the world that liberalism
is treason. †

In these quotations, as throughout the literature of the extreme right, the
connection between liberalism, socialism and communism is made clear. Thus,
if few avowed socialists and virtually no Communist Party members can be
found in the United States, the rightist has the duty of attacking the liberals, for
the welfare state that they seek is really the same as communism anyway. And,
by extension, virtually all the causes the liberals support are tainted, and thus
must be opposed.

Problems at Home and Abroad

With communism so close to victory in the world and so completely in
control of the American government, the extreme rightist has worries enough
for any man. Still, he manages to find time to concern himself with a host of
specific issues, for communism is on the march everywhere.

International Affairs

In this realm, all American policies since the recognition of the Soviet Union
are seen as disastrous.

> Our diplomatic war against communism has already been lost by bunglers
> or traitors within our own government. Our enemies have been strengthened
> through unnecessary lend lease and foreign aid arrangements.* *

These foreign policy setbacks are not simple mistakes.

> There is developing within our nation and the world a clear story of treason,
> that men in high places, not only here, but abroad, are being manipulated by
> powerful forces to do things that smack of cowardice and genuine betrayal.
> Look about you in the world. The Communists win every battle they engage in.
> Every decision of the United Nations, every action of the United States, and
> most free nations, seems to help advance the cause of aggressive—godless
> Communism. [Hargis, p. 7.]

Even apparent victories, like that of President John Kennedy over Premier Nikita
Khrushchev during the Cuban missile crisis of 1962, are viewed as defeats.

> When the facts of this squandered opportunity penetrate the minds of the
> American people, the realization will come that instead of "victory," October
> 22nd [the day the USSR said it would take its missiles out of Cuba] marked
> one of the most staggering diplomatic setbacks in American history
> . . . The last four years have seen our national policy-makers steadily de-
> stroying the world image of a strong, resolute and proud United States. Such
> lamb-like passivity in the face of insults by political midgets, such hesitation

---

†*Right* (May, 1956), quoted in Ralph E. Ellsworth and Sarah M. Harris, *The Amer-*
ican Right Wing (Washington, D.C.: Public Affairs Press, 1956), p. 34.

** "A Short History of the Minutemen," quoted in Thomas C. Lynch, Attorney General
of California, "Para-Military Organizations in California" (Sacramento: 1965), p. MM2.

to unleash our terrific military power when our basic security is in danger, is a far cry from the old America that we have revered. Something potent and valiant seems to have gone out of the American character, as reflected in our rulers, after two generations of wavering "Liberal" leadership in Washington. *

The implication that America should utilize her "terrific military power" —including atomic weapons—in foreign situations is one side of the rightist coin. The other is that if she doesn't, the United States should stay out of the troubles of the world entirely.

If isolationists had had their way, the United States would not today be so entangled in the affairs of all nations on earth that every border conflict threatens to become an American war.

The traditional policy of political isolation made it possible for America to become a powerful citadel of freedom, a beacon of hope for all men everywhere. Why *not* return to that policy? †

Such isolation certainly means withdrawal from the United Nations; such a "one-world" plan must of necessity be communist-inspired. Even if the United Nations had not been making decisions favoring communism, it would still be worse than useless, for the very concept of such a world organization is wrong.

The U.N. has been morally bankrupt from the beginning. It is impossible to adopt a charter that says that its member nations are "to practice tolerance and live together in peace with one another as good neighbors" and to include the Communists who know nothing of tolerance and whose program for peace is world victory for socialism. . . .

The ideological conflict is between the East and the West—slavery versus freedom, Communism versus capitalism, socialism versus Christianity, Satan versus God! In whichever realm one considers the conflict it is irreconcilable. The Bible says that we cannot walk together except they be agreed. The cold war makes a "United Nations" impossible. * *

Finally, there is the desire to break diplomatic and trade relations with communist countries, for there is no getting along with such evil. What's more, peaceful coexistence is a sham.

. . . The belief is widespread—and the official foreign policy of the United States reflects it—that Communist governments are not necessarily a menace to the freedom of this country or to the peace of the world, and that it is entirely possible for such a Communist government under proper leadership to be a peaceful orderly and constructive member of international society. . . .

The transparent falsehood of these popular and official misconceptions concerning Communism and Communist governments is now covered by a crust of complacent indifference on the part of a great majority of the Amer-

---

* Harold Lord Varney, "Cuba—The Truth" (New York; n.d.), p. 3.
† *Dan Smoot Report* (Dec. 28, 1964), 412.
** Carl McIntire, "A Bankrupt United Nations" (Collingwood, N.J.: n.d.), 1, 5.

ican people, which is overlaid with an inordinate passion for what is represented as "peace" and what President Eisenhower so frequently calls the "unthinkable horror" of another war.

If we have deliberately lost the will to resist Communist conquest of this country, then we should quit going through expensive motions to the contrary [defense and foreign aid spending], which only adds the vice of hypocrisy to the sin of surrender.*

Domestic Affairs

Extreme rightists may be ready to throw up their hands in despair at America's foreign policy, but they become, if possible, even more upset over the state of things here at home. The far right is sure the enemy knows that to have America fall into his hands without a fight, all that is necessary is to weaken the moral fiber of its people to change the old American way of doing things, to substitute collectivist values for individualism, to confuse and brainwash the people until they can no longer think or make decisions for themselves.

Individual responsibility for morals, saving and education are products of religion, the family, the schools and business. Therefore, Russian propaganda will be directed towards proving that religion is not true, that the family should be broken up, that the schools should not educate—only play, in what is called "progressive education," and business should not make a profit but go broke.†

One might wonder how Russian propaganda could have such an effect in the United States, since such a minuscule number of Americans read Russian publications. The answer is that the rightist believes the American press to be backing communism. "For the most part, America's daily newspapers are promoting the Communist line." [Hargis, p. 22.] One pamphlet declares: "The destructionists have been clever. They have gotten control of most of the media of mass communication—newspapers, radio, TV, book publishing, magazines, even newsstands and libraries."** Not only the mass media, but other sources of information are infested with Communists. "We employ its agents in the teaching profession, allowing them to work on the fertile minds of youth seeking a champion to pit against a scapegoat. They infest the entertainment media."***

Youth is a special target of the communists. "One of the objectives of the Communist conspiracy is to undermine the morals of our youth. It is easier to take over a country if the people's moral standards have been destroyed." ††

Manion Forum (Jan. 8, 1961), 3.

†Joe Crail, "A Businessman's Look at Communism vs. Capitalism," (Los Angeles: n.d.), 8.

**"A Call to Action to Every Real American."

***General Edwin A. Walker in *Hearings Before the Special Preparedness Subcommittee of the Committee on Armed Services*, United States Senate, 87th Congress, Sess. II, p. 1409.

††Rev. Paul C. R. Peterson, newsletter of Awake America for Christ (March, 1966).

An important part of the program of destruction takes place in the schools, through new theories of education. The title of one book sums up the whole extremist attitude towards the schools today: *Progressive Education is REDucation.** Though the underlying theories of "progressive education" were developed by an American, John Dewey, he is written off as a communist, and his ideas are seen as alien.

> So-called "liberals," "progressives," and "social reformers" generally are chang-
> ing the face of America after the Soviet pattern, including the face of the Amer-
> ican educational system. . . .
>
> The Communists are well-along with their plan to subvert American
> schools and American youth, from the kindergartens on through the elemen-
> tary grades to the colleges and universities. Some say there is a Communist
> cell on every college and university campus in the nation. . . . The Communists
> within the American educational system are not only "egghead intellectuals,"
> but the hardest of the hard-core Communists, who are unshakable in their
> conviction that American youth must be reshaped into the ugly pattern of the
> Soviet Union. [Hargis, pp. 60, 62, 64.]

Other ways of undermining youth include the introduction of pornography (such as books by J. D. Salinger and John Steinbeck) into literature classes and the promotion of rock-and-roll music, which is thought to be an essential part of the communist program.

> Also included in their [the communists'] ingeniously conceived master music
> plan are America's teenagers. . . . The music designed for high school students
> is extremely effective in aiding and abetting demoralization among teenagers,
> effective in producing degrees of artificial neurosis and preparing them for
> riot and ultimately revolution to destroy our American form of government
> and the basic Christian principles governing our way of life.
>
> The music has been called a number of things, but today it is best known
> as rock 'n' roll. . . .†

Even more dangerous in the eyes of the right is the new combination of the dangerous beat of rock 'n' roll with the potentially dangerous lyric of folk music. . . .

> The synthesis could well spell the doom of the United States of America,
> for no nation can long endure with its younger generation singing itself into
> defeatism, pessimism, peace-at-any-price mentality, disarmament, surrender,
> fear of death, hatred toward the South, atheism, immorality and the negation
> of patriotism. [Noebel, p. 212.]

The activities of the Supreme Court provide another sore point in domestic affairs for members of the far right, closely related at times to the supposed demoralization of American youth.

---

*Kitty Jones and Robert L. Olivier (Boston: 1956).
†Rev. David A. Noebel, *Rhythm, Riots and Revolution* (Tulsa, Okla.: Christian Crusade, 1966), p. 17.

Under the pretext of protecting freedom of religion, the Supreme Court has destroyed the freedom of millions of school children to recognize, or even learn about, the Source whence the liberties of our people came. Pretending to enforce a separation of church and state, the court has illegally assumed authority to banish from public schools all established faiths and forms of worship, and has, in effect, decreed agnosticism as the officially-approved religion of the United States. A small minority of children in school may discuss the doctrines of atheism, proclaim themselves agnostics, show irreverence toward God, or even blaspheme His name; but the preponderant majority of children who want spiritual nourishment may not speak a word to God. *

The prayer decision of the Supreme Court was deplorable, but it was probably no more than could be expected from Earl Warren and his fellow jurists, who in the eyes of the right have done more for the communists than any other branch of government. The court's heinous decisions began with the desegregation ruling in 1954.

By that decision the Supreme Court handed to the central government a power it had never before possessed—the power to put its grasping and omnipotent hand into a purely local function. . . . It will not be long before the socialist revolutionaries have what they want—control by the central government of what to teach and what not to teach. . . †

Other decisions have been as bad.

In the past three years the Supreme Court has issued at least fifteen decisions designed to put the meddling fingers of the federal politicians further into state affairs, and to completely break down all our defenses against the communist conspirators in our midst. . . .

Along with this has gone a continuation of the practice of the Roosevelt-packed Court in taking from the states and their citizens control over their own resources and their own livelihood. In 1954 . . . the court seized from the southwestern states control of natural gas production. Today it is natural gas; tomorrow it could be your corner grocery store or filling station—or local newspaper. [Gordon, pp. 19, 24.]

With such views there is little wonder that the right united in a drive to impeach Earl Warren.

The Supreme Court's actions are seen as only part of a general grab for power being perpetrated in America by the federal government. Fearing for the individual's sanctity, rightists oppose big government and the programs that create it. They wish to abolish income tax ("the root of all evil"), do away with Social Security and other trappings of the welfare state.* *All areas of government activity are seen as an attempt to increase federal power. Thus a civil

---

Dan Smoot Report (March 2, 1964), 65.

†Rosalie M. Gordon, *Nine Men Against America* (New Rochelle, N.Y.: n.d.), p. 14.

**Another book in the Insight Series, *The Welfare State: Who Is My Brother's Keeper?* by Fred Krinsky and Joseph Boskin, explores this controversy further.

rights bill is thought to have little to do with helping the plight of the American Negro. Typical of the reactions to the proposed Civil Rights Bill of 1964 is the following:

> The results of this legislation would be enormous suffering by, and oppression of, both our white citizens and our Negro citizens alike; and such turmoil, rioting, bitterness and chaos as benefits only the Communists—or a federal govment drunk with its drive for power.*

In general the extreme right does not concern itself much with the plight of Negroes, though it does try to eschew racism. Still, some see a historical justification for segregation.

> So far as the Bible is concerned, there has never been a more segregated people in the history of the world than the Children of Israel. The Old Testament demanded it of them. This segregation was based upon race, religion and ethnical origin. †

Others find the whole race question a bogus one, created by the communists:

> If there is a mutual problem which needs solving with respect to the American Negro and the American White people, the patriotic Christian American leaders of the two races are quite capable of working it out. Neither the Negro people nor the White people have stirred up the racial segregation controversy in the South. The infamous "social crisis" is but another of the expensive, damaging, diversionary, and subversive actions of that breed of people within our midst who thrive on hate. They are the envious Communists, the pro-Communists, the fellow-travelers, the so-called "liberals" and "progressives," and the "social reformers," who are under compulsion to reshape America after the example of the Soviet Union. [Hargis, p. 98.]

In this world of the extremist, the communists are doing even more than capturing control of the American government and fomenting hatred between races otherwise living amicably together. The enemy is also felt to be utilizing many subtle methods in undermining America. Among the most diabolical, the rightist feels, are those that come disguised as medical programs and hygienic measures.

> Water containing Fluorine (rat poison—no antidote) is already the only water in many of our army camps, making it very easy for saboteurs to wipe out an entire camp personal [sic]. If this happens, every citizen will be at the mercy of the enemy—already within our gates. * *

> Parents were warned to keep their children away from the Salk polio shots. ... Most parents don't realize that the school children of today represent our Army and Navy ten years from now. If millions of them can be innoculated, let's say with radioactive substance that will cause cancer in a few years, why ten years from now the communists could walk in and take over our nation of old men. ††

---

*Sample John Birch Society advertisement, *JBS Bulletin* (March, 1964), 24.
†Carl McIntire, "The National Council of Churches, 1957" (Collingwood, N.J.: 1961), 29.
**Keep America Committee, leaflet.
††*Free Men Speak*, quoted in Ellsworth and Harris, *American Right Wing*, p. 16.

More than subversion through drugs, the extreme rightist has come to fear mental health programs. In 1956 there was great concern that a land grant to Alaska to support a mental health hospital would become a "Siberia U.S.A." where people who objected to the "collectivist" trend of American politics would be sent. More recently concern has been with federal mental health programs.

> We have been under a constant barrage of warnings . . . that the mental health of the nation is bad, and getting progressively worse. . . .
> Much of the fear engendered in the minds of the American people has an ulterior Communist motive behind it. This "phony" concern about our so-called declining "mental health" has been planted by Communist agents, fronters and sympathizers for the purpose of demoralizing the American people and spreading defeatism. As part of the Kremlin's psychological warfare, this negative propaganda is calculated to destroy our morale, thereby rendering us ineffective, and making us easy prey for the Red vultures. . . .
> This systematic and diabolical scheme to destroy the moral fibre of people and nations is being carried on right now in this country by highly trained and disciplined secret Soviet and American Red agents. Through the "professional cells" of the Communist Party, Reds are funnelling their conspirators into our Social, Health, Welfare, Church and Educational fields. Very coyly these Red vermin and their sympathetic allies are inculcating in the minds of the American people, especially our students, the idea that belief in God, love of country, family, and the American way of life denotes something wrong, psychologically speaking. As usual in most of their crafty schemes, the Reds are aided and abetted in their psychological warfare by Communist fronters, professional self-seekers, political opportunists and high society do-gooders.*

In the writings of the far right the struggle in the world is pictured most often as that between communism and Christianity, between Satan and God. But even some of the houses of God are tainted, for not unnaturally, the communists have infiltrated churches. A major complaint has been the intrusion of social issues, considered irrelevant by the rightist, into religion. The biggest offender in this regard has been the National Council of Churches.

> The Council has aided the Communist cause and sided with Russia on point after point in the cold war. It has been a spokesman for socialism, advocated federal aid to education, opposed states rights, stimulated racial strife in the country, promoted the welfare state. . . . †

The problem, as the rightist sees it, is that the "social gospel" has emptied Christianity of its spiritual content. And it was the revolutionary leader Lenin who ordered the communists to undermine the churches from within, by using the "social gospel."

---

*Keep America Committee, leaflet.
† *Free Men Speak*, quoted in Ellsworth and Harris, *American Right Wing*, p. 16.

... if you will strain all spiritual content out of Scripture, you can break religion's hold upon the people: God is changed from an all-powerful, all-knowing, and very personal heavenly Father—into some kind of vague, undefined universal force. Jesus is no longer a Deity—God himself. Jesus becomes merely a great man, a teacher, a philosopher, a social reformer.

A church establishment built on such notions as these is not an insurmountable obstacle in the path of the socialist revolution. On the contrary, it has become a very useful instrument for promoting socialism.

Many modern liberal ministers seem to have lost confidence in God. They react to problems around them by exerting pressure, in the name of Christian churches, for federal laws which will impose their notions of equality and morality on the entire nation. . . .

. . . . The language of modern liberalism is so similar to the language of communism; the root ideas of socialism are so closely akin to contemporary doctrines of the social gospel—that many cannot tell the difference.*

Solutions

In spite of the dire state of the world and the United States, the extreme degree of communist infiltration, the closeness of Russian victory, the people of the extreme right are not without hope that America can be saved.

... at least 95 per cent of all the human beings, on both sides of the Iron Curtain, *do not want Communism.* The job is not to unsell a majority from something they want or think is good for them, but to enable a *preponderant* majority to resist and refuse something they do not want. [Welch, p. 73.]

To help the majority defeat the worldwide conspiracy it is necessary for conscientious patriots to join the fight.

Enlist in this war—the outcome of which will determine whether your children and your children's children will *live* in Freedom, or be ground to death under the iron heel of a bloody, atheistic communist tyrant. †

To the rightist, one cannot take part in this war simply by working through existing political parties, for both national organizations have been captured by the enemy.

There has not been one presidential election since World War II where the American public has had an opportunity to vote for a real American. There have been times when the candidates were built up by big public relations campaigns that sold them to the American people but when they were once in office they failed to act in their nation's best interest. . . . In each case the people have merely had the opportunity to vote for whoever they thought might be the lesser of two evils.* *

Dan Smoot Report (Dec. 16, 1963), 397–398.
†"A Call to Action to Every Real American."
**"A Short History of the Minutemen," quoted in Lynch, p. MM3.

The solution to this dilemma is different for various organizations. Usually it includes joining the organization, studying books, pamphlets and periodicals exposing the communist menace, spreading the gospel of Americanism to acquaintances, writing letters to Congressmen and other officials, setting up front organizations, infiltrating PTA's and library boards to Americanize curricula and placing conservative books on the shelves, harassing pro-communist and liberal speakers, patronizing companies favorable to rightists, boycotting stores that sell goods made in communist countries, attempting to capture control of political parties at the local level, and voting for conservative candidates.

Some militant rightists however, believe that these sorts of actions are totally useless. With apocalyptic vision they feel Americans must arm themselves and prepare to defeat communism by force of arms in the United States.

> . . . the objectives of the Minutemen are to abandon wasteful, useless efforts and to begin immediately to prepare for the day when Americans will once again fight in the streets for their lives and their liberty. We feel there is overwhelming evidence to prove that this day must come. [*Ibid.*]

Chapter Two

The Right Speaks for Itself

The far right is more than a series of intellectual positions on the political and religious problems of today. Like all vital social movements, its dynamic derives from an emotional reaction to a changing world, and strong emotions suffuse the writings of its adherents. To savor this aspect of the right, to get the feel of the emotional stance and motives of its members, it is necessary to listen to its spokesmen at greater length.

In the following selections some of the leading figures on the extreme right speak for themselves. As will become quickly apparent, the tone of their words is often one of nostalgia for an earlier time when the world seemed simpler, when people seemed to know right from wrong, when patriotism and traditional faith were unquestioned and shared by all. Extremists are both angered and terrified by the fact that America has changed from the untroubled society they think it once was to one that has become too complex and relativistic in its beliefs. This longing for a simpler life, coupled with extreme anger at those they think have caused the changes, and an apocalyptic vision of approaching Armageddon, are most characteristic of rightist minds. In the following writings these important emotional components of the far right world view can be seen, and perhaps linked to attitudes that are common among most Americans.

Americanism versus Amorality

Robert Welch

Born in 1899 in North Carolina, Robert Welch was educated at his state university, the U.S. Naval Academy, and Harvard Law School. He rose to become vice president of a large candy manufacturing firm and a leader of the National Association of Manufacturers. In 1957 he began to devote almost his full time to anti-communist activities. *The Blue Book,* from which these selections are taken, is a publication of Mr. Welch's spoken presentation to a small group of men in Indianapolis in 1958—a meeting that was the founding of the John Birch Society. The book has since gone to at least fourteen printings.

Now, gentlemen, in looking thoroughly and realistically at the danger to everything we have inherited, spiritual as well as material, and at the cause of that danger, we come to the second of the fundamental reasons for deep and basic anxiety. And putting that matter bluntly at once, the reason is simply loss of faith. Not just loss of faith in God and all his works but loss of faith in man and his works too, in his reasons for existence, in his purposes, and in his hopes.

Now I know that there are still millions of devout Catholics, fundamentalist Protestants, and faithful Jews in this country who still believe unquestioningly in the divine truths and powers which their Bibles reveal to them, and whose conduct and relations with their fellow men are guided strictly by the precepts of their religious faith—or who at least feel that they have sinned whenever they have transgressed such precepts as understood by their consciences. I have hundreds of good friends in those categories, including some in this room.

Let all of us thank whatever God we severally worship that there is so large a remnant of the really true believers still left. We honor them. We need their steadying adherence to the rock of reverence, and their aspiration of unwavering obedience to ancient and divine commandments. We desperately need their unshakable confidence in absolutes, in eternal principles and truths, in a world of increasing relativity and transitoriness in all things. We admire them. In fact, as will become more clear tomorrow, the young man I admire most of all of those America has produced was a fundamentalist Baptist missionary named John Birch. My own obsession with this fight against the increasing forces of evil in the world, which—as already explained—has caused me to give up business carrer and income and any prospect of ever having any peace or leisure again during my lifetime, is due in large part to my admiration for John Birch; to my feeling that I simply had to pick up and carry, to the utmost of my ability and energy, the torch of a humane righteousness which he was carrying so well and so faithfully when the Communists struck him down.

· ·

We must not only know the truth, but face the truth, if it is to set us free or to keep us so. And the fundamental truth of our times, gentlemen, as distinguished from the fundamentalist truth, is just this. Except for the diminishing number of fundamentalists of all religions, and the increasing but still comparatively small percentage of the human race which has fervently accepted Communism as a religion, all faith has been replaced, or is rapidly being replaced, by a pragmatic opportunism with hedonistic aims. And what a fall that is for a race which can boast of once having listened to a St. Augustine, a St. Francis of Assisi, a John Milton, or an Alfred Tennyson. The further and more specific manifestation of that fundamental truth is that *in Western Europe and America today we are living in a spiritual vacuum*, exactly as were the Romans after they had lost any real faith in their pagan gods and before the rise of Christianity.

In the middle of the nineteenth century Lord Tennyson, with one of the greatest and most rational minds, at the very apex of the enlightenment achieved by the Western European Civilization, could still write with complete conviction:

> Our little systems have their day;
>   They have their day and cease to be:
>   They are but broken lights of thee,
> And Thou, O Lord, art more than they.

Compare that with the acutely cynical flippancy of a current gem, which goes something as follows:

> A life force afflicted with doubt,
> As to what its own being was about,
>   Said: "The truth I can't find,
>   But I'm creating a mind,
> Which may be able to figure it out.

And in that comparison you can see the magnitude of our loss, as to a base for our morals, our purposes, and our aspirations.

For the next part of the truth we must face is that for the past several hundred years our morality, in Europe and America, was tied to a belief in the rewards and punishments delineated by Christian dogma; to the accepted commandments of a very real and very majestic deity; and to the desire of the true believer to become worthy of the love of an omniscient living God. The reality and earnestness of Christian faith was the foundation of our ethics, and the substance of our consciences.

When Voltaire said that if God did not exist we should have to invent him, it was a very blasphemous remark but a very penetrating one, as to the dependence at that time of morals, humanitarianism, and purposes on what has since come to be called the anthropomorphic conception—that is, a God in whose image man himself was created.

. . . .

Through many centuries Christianity, despite all of its splits and schisms, supplied the fabric of morality for the whole Western World —through its threats of punishments, promises of rewards, and the humanizing effect of its proffered love by and for a Divine Father. But despite all the billions of words that have been written to the contrary, that fabric is now pierced and torn and weakened beyond needed dependability. For a vast majority of those who proclaim themselves Christians today, and attend church services, do not really and literally believe in either the punishments, the rewards, or even in the physical and biological existence of a Divine Father with any interest in their personal lives and actions. The momentum of a former belief, and the customs which grew out of it, still have great value. But the fabric is worn too thin to have its old effectiveness.

Now please do not jump to any conclusions that I want to see Christianity denied, discarded, or even further weakened, in the slightest. Exactly the opposite is true, as I hope to make clear when we come back to this subject from the constructive side tomorrow. But I am not in favor of trying to reimpose all or any of the strands of a fundamentalist faith on those whose reason, whether right or wrong, has honestly told them that we cannot know such positive things about the Unknowable. For that would be like trying to tie the waves of the ocean together with ropes, or to confine them with fishing nets.

But I believe there is a broader and more encompassing faith to which we can all subscribe, without any of us doing the slightest violation to the more specific doctrines of his own creed or altars of his own devotion. And I believe it is an ennobling conception, equally acceptable to the most fundamentalist Christian or the most rationalistic idealist, because its whole purport is to strengthen and synthesize the ennobling characteristics of each man and the ennobling impulses of his own personal religion. It is a conception which the Baptist John Birch, the Catholic Hilaire Belloc, and the agnostic Thomas Jefferson would alike have welcomed. And in the short time we can give to so mighty a subject, in this particular program, I shall return to it tomorrow to the extent necessary for its place in my immediate proposals. What I am trying to do now is merely to make a realistic appraisal of our weaknesses, because without doing so we can only dissipate our remaining strength in trying to build fortifications and temples on sinking mud or shifting sand.

For not only is this loss of reinforcing faith in the cement of our morals a weakness in itself of immense significance, but like all of our weaknesses it has been pounced upon by the Communists, and used and made worse by them with great skill and determination for their own purposes. When an individual American, or any other human being, sees himself as no longer responsible to a Divine Being, but as merely a living accident, not connected in any way with cosmological purpose, it becomes far easier for him to make his decisions about his own life and actions entirely on the basis of his temporal comforts and the earthly desires of his own personality. If he is the kind of man that wants financial success for the ease, or leisure and travel, or the prestige which it supposedly brings (and sometimes does), he is not going to buck Communist pressures in any way that will endanger that success or handicap his progress. If he is imbued with ambition for power, he is more readily inclined to get on the Communist bandwagon, if that seems to be the surest *road* to power (as it certainly does to a great many Americans today). The Communists are able to use this lack of moral stamina among their enemies in a thousand ways to make their own progress easier and the conquest of those enemies more rapid.

The most terrible result of this collapse of the rock of faith on which our morality was built is the rise of the amoral man—of which the usual Communist himself is the most illustrative example. For an amoral man, like Stalin, is infinitely worse, from the point of view of a humanitarian civilization, than an immoral one like Hitler. An immoral man may lie, steal, and murder; the worst of them even without any seeming limit or hesitation. But it hurts his conscience. He is, at least potentially, susceptible to humanitarian or moral considerations, to some extent, and if they are presented cogently enough to him. There is even the possibility always that he may sometime, or in some ways, repent and make what amends he can for his crimes.

An amoral man, however, has simply wiped out his conscience, along with any reason for its existence. He is not immoral, even when performing coldblooded mass murders, because to him there is no such thing as either morality or immorality. There is only the pragmatic consideration of the advantages or disadvantages to himself, for his own personal desires or plans, in any action—whether it be the building of a monument or the murder of his wife. And these amoral men, the products of a materialistic and sophomoric disillusionment, who have not yet gone on in their thinking to deeper and more permanent truths, now stalk in our midst in greater numbers than ever before in history. Such men, among the Communists, and they are plentiful and highly placed, have no real dedication even to Communism. They regard it merely as an expedient means to satisfy their personal ambitions more nearly than would any other star to which they might hitch their wagons.

But on our own side of the fence, among the millions who either are, or pretend to be, non-Communists, the amoral man, who has no slightest inner concern with right or wrong, is one of the greatest causes of our constant retreat, and one of the greatest dangers to our survival. And he doesn't wear any label. He usually lives up to the appearance of excellent morals, because it is expedient for his purposes, and you will usually find him in church on Sunday morning, maybe even a Catholic church. But as a member of the United States Senate, running for the presidency, and smart enough to know the strong Communist support behind-the-scenes which he will have to get in order to have any chance of being nominated in 1960, such an amoral man can do a tremendous amount of ball-carrying on behalf of the Communist aims here in the United States; and he can do an almost equal amount of damage to anti-Communist morale in other parts of the world, by his well-publicized speeches against Chiang Kai-shek or in favor of the Algerian rebels. Or an amoral man, as the head of a great so-called Republic, may have no slightest scruples or concern about its fate or the fate of other nations, in the face of Communist conquest and of the cruel tyranny of their rule. And any similarity of characters in this story to any living persons is not coincidental.

. . . .

. . . As important and absolutely vital as our stopping the Communists has become, and as much as our loss of moral fibre is now deliberately made more rapid and more damaging by the Communists for their present and future purposes, even throwing the Communists completely out of the picture would not stop the fatal deterioration in our sense of values which is now in process. Besides the short-term job of eliminating the Communist danger—and Herculean as that job may be, it has to be done in a short term or it can't be done at all—we have the equally important longer-range job of ending this mass psychological flight towards amorality; and of restoring convincing reasons for men once again to strive to live up to moral and humanitarian ideals. Otherwise, there is no chance of saving our Christian-style civilization from self-destruction; and it will merely go down to chaos, and the ultimate serfdom of the weak under the strong, more lingeringly than if it is destroyed and its once-free members are enslaved by the Communists.

But whereas stopping the disease of collectivism is a matter of honest diagnosis and drastic surgery, this equally gigantic problem is one of restoration rather than of removal. We have to find something to live for, gentlemen, that is greater than ourselves, or we surely fall back from the semi-civilized level of existence, which man has laboriously achieved, into a moral jungle and its inevitably concomitant intellectual darkness. I tried to put the picture of where we are heading in a sonnet to my good friend Alfred Noyes about a year ago—and fortunately a few months before he died. Because it summarizes, as concisely and as expressively as I know how, the outlook I have been trying to define, I am asking your leave to read it at this point.

To Alfred Noyes

As after Rome, now once again the drapes
    Of ignorance and bigotry and lust
    May close upon the scene. Insentient dust
Will bury the forgotten stage. And apes
Who know not man, his glory and his dreams,
    His wish to be more worthy of his God,
    Will stalk the earth and wield the brutal rod,
And stamp upon each tiny light that gleams.
Amid the dull collective monotone
    Of universal serfdom will be lost
The memory of song and singer. Prone
    And helpless, soon, upon the rubbish tossed,
Will die the Muse. Let us rejoice to own
    This one great poet more before the holocaust.

And it is not only the muse of poetry that will die of abuse and neglect, if man's loss of faith in there being anything in the universe worth while except his appetites is permitted to continue. But we do not have to let it continue. Before our very eyes lie all the incentives man needs to set him back on the road of striving towards moral perfection, true intellectual greatness, civilized relationships, and eternal hope for a still better and greater future, which seemed to him to be such natural goals a hundred years ago. Making those incentives understood, and giving contemporary man a renewed faith in himself, in his destiny, and in a still greater God than was recognized and worshipped by his ancestors, is a task for myriads of dedicated individuals over generations of time. We can only contribute all we are able to its proper beginning. But without such a goal and purpose all of our efforts simply to stop Communism, or to destroy an ephemeral conspiracy of gangsters, are not only doomed to failure. Even if successful they would but postpone the days of darkness for our children, for their children, and for a race of men that once knew the light.

We shall return to the constructive side of this need and this undertaking in the morning.

. . . . `. . . .

The greatest enemy of man is, and always has been, government. And the larger, the more extensive that government, the greater the enemy.

Now clearly the United States which, throughout its early centuries, was the greatest beneficiary from the scarcity of government that the world has ever known, should not only return to the right course for its own further growth in prosperity, freedom, and happiness, but should set an example again for the whole world. In fact, the word *americanist*, with a small *a*, should be made, and become understood, as the very antithesis of socialism, and communism with a little *c*. For the *communist*—using the word now with a little *c* to denote a theoretician rather than a member of the conspiracy—the communist believes that a collectivist society should swallow up all individuals, make their lives and their energies completely subservient to the needs and the purposes of the collectivist state; and that any means are permissible to achieve this end. The true *americanist* believes that the individual should retain the freedom to make his own bargain with life, and the responsibility for the results of that bargain; and that means are as important as ends in the civilized social order which he desires. The same two words, with initial capitals, Communists and Americanists, should merely denote the aggressive fighters for these two mutually exclusive philosophies.

But Americanism, as either a phrase or a force on the contemporary world scene, has been eroded into something negative and defeatist. It has come to represent merely a delaying action against the victorious march of its enemy, collectivism. The air is full of clarion calls to Americans to organize, in order better to fight against socialism, communism, or some vanguard of their forces.

Twice each day the mail brings to my desk pleas for me to contribute money, or effort, or moral support, or all three, to some group which is battling to hold back some particular advance of collectivist storm troops. Even those organizations or activities which bear a positive label are motivated by negative thinking. An association *for* the Bricker Amendment is, in reality, an association *against* the intervention of international socialist forces in the control of our domestic lives.

Americanism has become primarily a denial of something else, rather than an assertion of itself. And there are many of us who think that this should be true no longer. We think that Americanism should again come to mean, and to be, a positive, forward-looking pholosophy; a design and example of social organization which boldly and confidently offers leadership along the one hard but sure road to a better world.

It is not just in the United States, of course, that all the aggressiveness is on the side of the socialist–communist allies. In the world-wide ideological struggle which divides mankind today, we conservatives fight always on the defensive. The very name by which we identify ourselves defines our objective. It is to conserve as much as we can, out of all we have inherited that is worth while, from the encroachments and destructiveness of this advancing collectivism. We build no more icons to freedom; we merely try to fend off the iconoclast.

Such has been the pattern during the whole first half of the twentieth century. From the bright plateaux of individual freedom and individual responsibility, which man had precariously attained, there has been a steady falling back toward the dark valleys of dependence and serfdom. But this ignominious retreat has been just as true of Americans, the heirs of a strong new society, as of the tired residual legatees of an old and enfeebled European civilization. During this long and forced retreat we have fought only a rearguard and sometimes delaying action. We have never been rallied to counterattack, to break through the enemy or rout him, and to climb again beyond our highest previous gains. And in the unending skirmishes, to hold as much as possible of the ground currently occupied, we have lost all sight of the higher tablelands of freedom which once were our recognized goals. I for one, and many others like me, are no longer willing to consider only when to retreat and how far. There is a braver and a wiser course.

If we heirs of all the ages are to find a turning point in this rapid and sometimes stampeding descent, in which we are abandoning instead of improving our inheritance; if the last half of the twentieth century is to see the curve that measures individual dignity turn upward; if the men who really wish to be free and self-reliant are to begin climbing back up the mountainside; then the goal must be known, and the purpose of aggressive offense must replace defensive defeatism as the banner under which we march. It is fatal to be merely against losing ground, for then there is no way to go but back. We have to be for something; we must know what that something is; and we must believe it is worth a fight to obtain. Reduced to its simplest and broadest terms, that something is less government and more responsibility. For both less government and more responsibility bring increasing opportunities for human happiness.

Due to the tremendous momentum given us by our hardworking, ambitious, and individualistic forefathers, our nation is still by far the most dynamic in the world in its productive processes, and in its influences on the whole world's standard of living. We must again become equally dynamic in our *spiritual* influence; in our positive leadership and example to provide a governmental environment in which individual man can make the most of his life in whatever way *he*—and not his government—wishes to use it.

There are many stages of welfarism, socialism, and collectivism in general, but communism is the ultimate state of them all, and they all lead inevitably in that direction. In this final stage, communism, you have a society in which class distinctions are greater than in any other, but where position in these classes is determined solely by demagogic political skill and ruthless cunning. You have a society in which all those traits which have helped to make man civilized, and which our multiple faiths have classified as virtues, are now discarded as vices—while exactly their opposites are glorified. And you have a society in which every *fault* of government that we have discussed above is held to be a *benefit* and a desirable part of the framework of life.

But there is an exactly opposite direction. It leads toward a society in which brotherhood and kindliness and tolerance and honesty and self-reliance and the integrity of the human personality are considered virtues; a society which venerates those traits exactly because they have helped the human animal to achieve some degree of humanitarian civilization, and are the common denominators of all our great religions. This direction leads toward a governmental environment for human life founded on the basis of long experience with government; on experience which shows government to be a necessary evil, but a continuous brake on all progress and the ultimate enemy of all freedom. It is the forward direction, the upward direction—and americanism, I hope, shall become its name.

Why Not Return to the "Old Country"?*

Paul Harvey

Mr. Harvey broadcasts a daily national network radio program of news commentary.

Youngster, let me tell you what it was like in the Old Country.

Once, milkin' an old cow in the back barnlot, I got tired of her swattin' me in the face with a tail full of cockleburrs. So, with a piece of binder twine, I tied her tail to my leg. I hadn't gone around the barn but about four times before I realized my mistake.

We had fun in the Old Country, though. We played darts with a corncob. It had three chicken feathers in one end and a nail in the other. But if I picked the wrong target, like the sugar sack drainin' cottage cheese on the clothes line, Mom would likely thump me on the head with her thimble finger.

So we didn't have much of what you'd call juvenile crime in the Old Country. Oh, every farm boy had to try smokin' corn silk or grapevine once—until he got a mouthful of toasted ants—or until he got caught and got stropped. And the grocer might fill the apple basket with the best ones on top. But we didn't concentrate on learnin' the tricks of a trade; we learned the trade.

And stealing things or hurting people was almost unheard of in the Old Country.

And religion and education were all so mixed up together when I was a boy you couldn't tell where one left off and the other began. Patriotism was taught in every school class every day. Our national heroes were honored, almost revered.

Political speeches and religious sermons and civic celebrations always rang with patriotic fervor. Soldiers were somebody. Civil servants were servants, not masters.

Freeloading was a disgrace. Ice cream was homemade. And marriage was forever. . . .

In the Old Country.

A farmer could plant anything he liked any place he wanted on his

---

*From *Human Events* (September 7, 1963), 10. Copyright 1963 by General Features Corporation. Reprinted with the kind permission of the publisher.

own land. Folks who worked harder were rewarded for it, so everybody worked harder.

Most everybody had one idea about life: to leave the woodpile a little higher than he found it. And most everybody did. We had no card-carrying Communists; we had Cross-carrying Christians . . . in the Old Country. We told dialect jokes and everybody laughed, because all of us were "mostly something else," in the Old Country.

It isn't there anymore.

I am a displaced person, though I never left my homeland.

I am a native-born American. I never left my country. It left me.

The Faith of Our Fathers*

Billy James Hargis

Billy James Hargis was born in 1929 and ordained a minister at the age of eighteen. After some years with pastorates in Missouri and Oklahoma, he became interested in the problem of communist influence in America, particularly within Protestant churches. He resigned a pastorate about 1950, and soon his Christian Crusade movement was growing in numbers and financial resources by leaps and bounds. The Christian Crusade, centered in Tulsa, has sponsored speaking tours, radio programs, conventions and special schools, and numerous publications.

Our founding fathers did not intend to establish a government that did not recognize God and Jesus Christ, but instead, their vision was to establish government that did not recognize a church or an ecclesiastical body. †

Today, the left-wingers and liberals, in far too many instances, interpret separation of church and state, as separation of state and God. This is the opposite of the original meaning of this great principle and doctrine.

---

*From Billy James Hargis, *Communist America: Must It Be?* (Tulsa, Okla.: Christian Crusade, 1960), pp. 31–37, 38–39. Reprinted with the permission of the author and publisher.

†*The Politics of Religion in America,* by Fred Krinsky, is another book in the Insight Series; the crucial issues of church–state relations are its central topic.

Patriotism and Christianity are very close to each other. It is impossible to be a true Christian and not be a true patriot. One who loves God also loves his country. Our forefathers believed in Jesus Christ and in His atoning blood. They talked about their faith in their homes, taught it in the schools as well as in the churches, and sang of it in wilderness brush arbors, tabernacles and camp-meetings.

Our forefathers followed the Biblical admonition of Jesus, "Seek ye first the Kingdom of God and His righteousness and all these other things shall be added unto you." They heeded the warning in Psalms 9:17, "The wicked shall be turned into hell and all nations that forget God." The American dream has had a progressive fulfillment because of the Christian faith of this nation, and because of the religious liberty graciously accorded all men, regardless of their beliefs.

Communism, however, has come along with insistance that America no longer look toward God, but instead toward government. Communism, through its associates, liberalism, progressivism, socialism, and modernism is creating class warfare within America, fomenting hatred, stirring up various so-called "social crises," destroying love of country, perverting morals of young and old, casting aside beloved traditions, banning the Bible from American schools, and in general reducing the proud and free American citizenship to an insignificant, helpless, hopeless pawn of giant government.

America is and always has been a Christian nation. The very spirit of the American Constitution reflects the teachings of Christ. America was founded by Christians. Every president to date, has been or professed to be a Christian, with perhaps one exception, Thomas Jefferson. The overwhelming majority of American citizens are members of the Christian faith, and these Christian citizens are paying 70 per cent of the nation's taxes.

The United States always has been a Christian nation, willing, ready and able to fight for the right of every man to worship as he pleases. The first constitutional form of government ever signed in all history was signed by forty-one of America's pilgrim fathers. Their laws were molded closely on the Bible. Freedom of divine worship was, for the first time, incorporated in the constitutional laws of a country. In fact, the primary objective of our founding fathers was the discovery and establishment of a land and a nation where they could worship God according to the dictates of their own consciences, and where they could establish homes and rear their children without fear of the iron hand of tyranny.

Never did the founding fathers of America intend that our government become one which denies God. Never did they intend for our government to "shield" our children from the saving knowledge of God's truth by banning the Bible and prayer from the public schools. The first great American president, George Washington, made it clear that it is impossible to govern the world without the Bible.

The Plymouth Colony Law for Education of Children states,

> ... the good education of children ... is of ... benefit to any commonwealth. It is ordered that the Deputies and Select men of every town shall have a vigilant eye to see that all parents and masters so duly endeavor, by themselves or others, to teach their children ... so much learning as through the blessings of God they may attain, at least to be able to read the Scriptures ... and in some competent measure to understand the ... principles of the Christian religion necessary to salvation. ...

"... the good education of children ... is of ... benefit to any commonwealth. It is ordered that the Deputies and Select men of every town shall have a vigilant eye to see that all parents and masters so duly endeavor, by themselves or others, to teach their children ... so much learning as through the blessings of God they may attain, at least to be able to read the Scriptures ... and in some competent measure to understand the ... principles of the Christian religion necessary to salvation. ..."

Such was the faith of our fathers—holy faith. They were true to that faith till death, and we hold the same privilege and responsibility. Never in all of America's glorious history has the faith of our fathers been dimmer in the hearts and souls of the sons and daughters of America as today.

The New England Articles of Confederation in 1643, stated, "... we all came into these parts of America with one and the same end and aim, namely to advance the Kingdom of our Lord Jesus Christ and to enjoy the liberties of the Gospel in purity with peace. ..."

Early American settlers signing the Rhode Island Compact in 1638, declared their faith in this manner: "We whose names are underwritten ... will submit our persons, lives, and estates unto our Lord Jesus Christ, the King of Kings and the Lord of Lords, and to all those perfect and absolute laws of His, given us in His holy word of truth, to be judged and guided thereby."

Our Declaration of Independence proclaims "reliance on the protection of Divine providence." The Thanksgiving Proclamation of the Continental Congress on November 1, 1777, spoke of pleasing God through the merits of Jesus Christ and of "the promotion and enlargement of the kingdom which consisteth in righteousness, peace, and joy in the Holy Ghost." The founders of America had no hesitation, and no shame in acknowledging the Bible as the word of God and as the guide for their nation and their nation's rulers.

The fifty-six courageous men who signed the Declaration of Independence, instantly became criminals in the eyes of the British Crown and were made to suffer untold hardships and persecutions because of their faith. The price of freedom was very great. Yet today, America is in deadly danger of losing its precious freedoms because millions upon millions of its free sons and daughters will not consider their danger nor arouse themselves to take personal and individual responsibility for the saving and preservation of those freedoms.

One of the Declaration signers was John Hart. His thirteen children fled their father's home for their lives; his wife died alone. His large farm was pillaged and his livestock driven away and destroyed. He was a hunted man. He paid a bitter price for freedom. Lewis Morris of New York, a wealthy man and a graduate of Yale University, wrote his name on the parchment. His forest of more than one thousand acres was burned, his home destroyed, and his family forced to flee for their lives. Richard Stockton of New Jersey, a Princeton graduate and lawyer, was arrested, thrown into prison, denied food, and given such brutal treatment that he never recovered his health. His papers and library were burned and his farm laid in ruins. Francis Lewis, another signer, saw his home plundered and wrecked, his business and source of income swept away, and everything he had confiscated.

Our founding fathers were willing to give all they had, even their lives, to obtain the freedoms which we now take for granted and which are gradually being cut away from us. American citizens have become far more interested in what they can get out of government than in what they can give to preserve their Republican form of government. The judgment of God surely will fall more severely upon America than upon other lands because much is required of those who have been granted much. Christian America has gained the most of all the civilized world and, if America falls, the fall of it will be great indeed. The suffering of American people under godless, satanic Communism, will be unparalleled in its horror, brutality and abandon.

Under Communism, no one as an individual can say, "My land, my farm, my home, my automobile, my cattle, or even my dog." As Congressman Wint Smith of Kansas has warned, "Under Communism you cannot possess anything except your picture with a card (with your serial number), your residence and the place where you work by government order. Of course, you would never say, 'This is my country,' because you belong to godless, atheistic, international Communism."

America has become a great nation because its great leaders and its people have believed in God, but godless leaders have infiltrated and subverted practically all phases of the American way of life. The people as a whole are being swept along by the socialists, the liberals, the progressives, the modernists, unwittingly making themselves tools as well as dupes of the international Communist conspiracy, which is active not only in America but in every nation and every land in the world. The end and aim of Communism is world conquest and world enslavement, with America being the grand prize of all.

Seldom are the sacred, patriotic songs of the land of the free such as "America," "The Star Spangled Banner," "America the Beautiful," "God Bless America," and "Faith of Our Fathers," sung in public meetings, colleges, theaters, or even churches anymore because those songs glorify God, bless God, thank God, and praise God "from whom all blessings flow."

In the famous Trinity Church decision of the American Supreme Court in February, 1892, Justice Brewer said, ". . . no purpose of action against religion can be imputed to any legislation, state or national, because this is a religious people." Christianity is and always has been a vital part of the American way of life and the American form of government. There is no other possible explanation for the blessing of America, for in all lands where religious freedom is denied the standard of living is extremely low in contrast with the United States. No nation which denies God has long prospered or endured.

Yet, little by little, decree by decree, America is denying God and turning its face away from the Saviour of the world. On June 10, 1955, the attorney general of California handed down an "opinion" that the Bible and prayer are unconstitutional in California's public schools. The opinion was given by Edmund G. "Pat" Brown, then attorney general, now governor of the state of California.

Mr. Brown said, "Daily prayer . . . might well be a disruptive element which would weaken the moral influence of parents and teachers." Such a view is quite in contrast to the view of the father of our country, George Washington, who said that "religion and morality" were "indispensable supports" for political prosperity, and that "reason and experience both forbid us to expect that national morality can prevail in exclusion of religious principle."

All too many other states have followed the example of California in banning the Bible from the public schools. Wherever the Bible is banned, sooner or later, the "Pledge of Allegiance to the Flag of the United States of America" and the displaying of the flag itself are also discreetly omitted. Thus, are love of God and love of country stifled in the young.

Are we ashamed of our nation? Are we ashamed of our flag? Are we ashamed of our God? Are we ashamed of the faith of our fathers?

America's greatest need in this dark and deadly hour is continuous, prevailing, intercessory prayer. God's divine prescription for the recovery of a nation is found in II Chronicles 7:14: "If my people, which are called by my name, shall humble themselves, and pray, and seek my face, and turn from their wicked ways; then will I hear from Heaven, and will forgive their sins, and will heal their land."

If God's people, which are called by His name, Christians, will remember the faith of their fathers, God will heal their land. America can be saved by doing the opposite to the will of Communists. Instead of turning away from God, turn toward God. As a matter of fact, the antidote to every Communist intrigue is to do the opposite, for all of Communism is based upon a lie.

. . . .

America is being sold out by treasonous, traitorous leaders. America is being surrendered to the enemy by a deceived people. America's salvation is an immediate return to the faith of our fathers, and the declaration of that faith in the Bible, the word of God. America must return to the faith which proudly declares, "I am not ashamed of the gospel of Christ for it is the power of God unto salvation to everyone that believeth."

America's destruction is in satanic Communism. America's salvation is in the faith of our fathers, in Jesus Christ, the Son of God.

The Decline of National Morale*

Ezra Taft Benson

Ezra Taft Benson was born in 1899. By profession a marketing specialist, he acted as Executive Secretary of the National Council of Farmer Cooperatives from 1939 to 1944, and was President Eisenhower's Secretary of Agriculture

*From Ezra Taft Benson, *The Red Carpet* (Salt Lake City, Utah: 1962), pp. 238–240, 296–298. Copyright 1962 by Bookcraft, Inc. Reprinted with the permission of the publishers.

during both administrations. Benson is an active leader of the Church of Jesus Christ of Latter-Day Saints.

. . . Some of you may have read, as I have, some of those great volumes by Will Durant as a part of "The Story of Civilization"—a monumental work. Volume Three impressed me very deeply. It is entitled *Caesar and Christ;* and records the rise and fall of the Roman Empire, and the coming of Christianity. It covers the time from 800 B.C. to 325 A.D., a period of 1125 years. Toward the end of the six hundred pages is one chapter, an epilogue, in which he tries to point out from what history reveals why this great Roman Empire fell. These are the major reasons. Note them carefully and try to determine in your mind if there is anything in evidence in our own country today which smacks of these causes, which this historian asserts were largely responsible for the fall of the great Roman Empire.

The first group of causes he lists as biological. These he considers the most fundamental. Mr. Durant claims they began with the educated classes, and started with the breakdown of the home and the family; the limitation of children; the refusal to assume the obligations of honorable parenthood; the deferment and avoidance of marriage. Sexual excesses were indulged in outside the marriage covenant. The practices of contraception and abortion became prominent, reduced fertility resulted. Sex ran riot and moral decay resulted.

Secondly, he mentioned the waste, among other things, of natural resources, mining, deforestation, erosion, neglect of irrigation canals. Most important he considered the negligence of harassed and discouraged men, the failure to teach high moral principles to the youth of the land—those principles which make for the building of character —and the sad neglect of our greatest single asset, our boys and girls.

Thirdly, he lists rising costs of government, armies, doles, public works, expanding bureaucracy, a parasitic court, depreciation of the currency, and absorption of investment capital by confiscatory taxation.

Is there anything suggestive in this summary?

The author listed other causes. Political causes, he said, were rooted in one fact, that through centralized control and the increasing despotism of the state, the citizens' civic sense was destroyed and dried up, thus destroying statesmanship at its source. Men felt powerless to express themselves and lost interest in government.

Yet, I presume, Rome has had no equal in the art of government. She achieved a democracy of free men and then destroyed it with corruption and violence.

I wonder what our founding fathers would do and say about America today if they were here. As they looked searchingly for the answers they would observe evidence of weak and vacillating leadership in many places, not confined to one group or one party. They would find a tendency for men in high places to place political expediency ahead of principle. They would be concerned with the alarming growth of a something-for-nothing philosophy, a failure of people to stand on their own feet. They would find some bad examples by unscrupulous politicians and by delinquent parents, and possibly a weakening of religious training, and the substitution therefore of a faith-destroying materialism.

As American citizens we need to rouse ourselves to the problems which confront us as a great Christian nation. We need to recognize that these fundamental, basic principles, moral and spiritual, lay at the very foundation of our achievements in the past. If we are to continue to enjoy our present blessings, we must have a return to these basic and fundamental principles. Economics and morals are both parts of one inseparable body of truth and they must be in harmony. We need to square our actions and our politics with these eternal principles.

. . . .

Along with greater emphasis on spirituality America needs a moral rejuvenation.

People who are willing—and we have some in this country—to trade freedom for security, are sowing the seeds of destruction and deserve neither freedom nor security. We have had for a good many years in evidence in this country, certain trends that strike, in my judgment, at the very foundation of much that we hold dear.

As nations tend to enjoy higher and higher standards of living, greater and greater comforts, greater and greater material blessings, there seems to be a tendency for them to become more and more interested in preserving their luxuries and their comforts than in preserving and safeguarding the ideals and principles that have made them great. In other words, there is a tendency for them to become infected with the germs of decadent morality.

In our own favored land, so richly blessed with material comforts, all is not well. We seem to be groping blindly, aimlessly, without finding the way. With all our material progress we have made no appreciable advances in human relations. Man still seems to be motivated largely by selfish interests without the power to control himself, his greed, his passions.

It seems clear as a people we have become indifferent, irreverent seekers after passing pleasures which have no permanent value. We have turned away from the eternal principles of righteousness.

In our rush for material things we have forgotten the God of this land. We claim to be a Christian nation, but we ignore the teachings of Christ. Religion seems to be a declining influence in the lives of our people.

Devotion in the home, which in the past has been such an anchor to youth, has all but vanished. Few families unite daily in family prayer and the reading of the scriptures.

One of the cardinal sins in our country is profanity—the taking of the name of our Lord in vain. Reverence for the name of Deity is enjoined in holy writ.

What of the Sabbath? Is not this day observed more as a holiday, a day of pleasure and indulgence with little thought for its sacredness? Would not a stranger in our land conclude that we consider this sacred law obsolete? We need the blessings which come from Sabbath observance.

What about our attitude as a nation regarding the sacred obligations of parenthood. No more sacred obligation has been placed upon men and women than that of honorable parenthood. We cannot escape the grave responsibility. The tragedy of broken homes—the breaking of the sacred bonds of holy matrimony on the least provocation is a national blot upon this great nation.

The divine law: "Thou shalt not commit adultery" is still in force. Sexual sin is next to murder in the category of crimes in the sight of God. Our record is such that it should have a sobering effect on all true Americans interested in the future welfare of this nation.

As a nation we need the refining and sustaining influences which come from obedience to divine law. Without such blessings the future of the nation is insecure. How can we expect divine acceptance when as a nation we are drunken through the staggeringly increased uses of intoxicating liquors, narcotics and tobacco. The increase in these vices weakens the moral fiber of our nation and brings disappointment and sadness followed by greater sins.

All these evidences are but the fruits of disobedience to divine injunction. Less obvious and more difficult to measure accurately are other evidences. We have become apathetic in our duty as citizens. The surprisingly low percentage of our people who exercise their right to vote for public officials is evidence of this fact.

There are also in evidence, in this blessed land, certain other trends which strike at the very foundation of all we hold dear. If permitted to go unchecked, and there seems to be little disposition to correct them, we might easily lose most of what we have gained during the past century and a half of our national existence.

It is my humble judgment that economics and morals are both parts of one inseparable body of truth and these must be in harmony. We must square our actions and our policies with eternal principles if this nation is to be preserved and not go the way of Rome and other dead civilizations. In no other way may we enjoy the continuing blessings of peace, prosperity and freedom.

The history of men and nations clearly teaches that only that nation is blessed "whose God is the Lord." God is still at the helm. He rules in the affairs of men and nations. As a nation we have been kept in the hollow of God's hand. But what of the future? In our history—ancient and modern—is the answer. Serve the God of this land who is Jesus Christ. There is no other course of safety. May we accept His guidance before it is too late. Real security can come in no other way.

The Red Roadblock*

Clarence Manion

Clarence Manion was born in 1896 and received an excellent education. As a Notre Dame law professor in the 1930's, Manion was also regarded as an important Indiana Democrat. During World War II, however, he began to oppose Democratic policies strongly, especially with respect to the Soviet Union. In 1952 he left his post as Dean of the Notre Dame Law School to become Chairman of the Commission on Inter-Governmental Relations under President Eisenhower. Resigning in 1954, he became active in anti-communist organizations. Since that time his Manion Forum has produced countless radio broadcasts and publications.

*From Clarence Manion, *The Conservative American* (Shepardsville, Ky.: Victor Publishing Co., 1966), pp. 190–195, 196–202. Copyright by Clarence Manion, 1966. Reprinted with the permission of the author and publisher. Some footnotes have been deleted.

Since the end of World War II, our foreign policy has been beleaguered by one—and only one—basic problem, namely, Communism. For twenty years we have been temporizing with the Communist menace instead of "coming to grips" with it as the first order of our moral and political duty. An elementary perception of the true nature of Communism clinches the conviction that we cannot coexist with it for the same reason that we cannot coexist with cholera, namely, that it is virulent, contagious and deadly. Official authorities on the disease called Communism, beginning with Karl Marx himself, have agreed that Communism will conquer everything that does not conquer Communism first, and the wide range of things that Communism is out to destroy certainly includes the United States of America. From 1917 to 1933 four successive Presidents of the United States perceived and acknowledged the predatory, amoral nature of Communism and the characteristic criminality of Communist dictators. Each of these Presidents concluded that agreements and diplomatic contacts with Communist governments were, therefore, worse than useless.

In 1920, our government announced officially that the Communist regime in Russia was "based upon the negation of every principle of honor and good faith, and every usage and convention underlying the whole structure upon which it is possible to base harmonious and trustful relations whether of nations or of individuals."[1]

This official 1920 conclusion by the United States government was publicly confirmed in 1963 by Alexei Adzhubei, son-in-law of Kremlin Premier Nikita Khrushchev. Mr. Adzhubei had just had a private audience with the late Pope John XXIII when newspapers asked the distinguished Communist emissary if he had discussed a possible agreement between the Kremlin and the Vatican. Mr. Adzhubei declared that no such agreement was contemplated because it would be useless. He was quoted by the reporters as follows:

> I am an atheist. I could break my word with the Holy Father. . . . As an atheist I would not be compelled to keep a promise. . . . There can never be peaceful co-existence between the Christian religion and our Communist doctrine.[2]

But in spite of our official discernment in 1920, frankly confirmed by Alexei Adzhubei forty-three years later, our government for thirty years has continued to negotiate agreements with the Kremlin which we have observed and which the Communists have broken at will. Since 1933, when President Roosevelt rescued the tottering Soviet

---

[1] Statement by Secretary of State Colby.
[2] Quoted by David Lawrence in the *Buffalo* (N.Y.) *Evening News* (March 22, 1963).

regime with American recognition, the Communist contagion has infected the entire human race while its ravage has paralyzed the freedom of one billion people now held in Communist slavery. Millions of these victims are now in the western hemisphere and high up on the agenda of the relentless Communist conquest are the Panama Canal Zone and Puerto Rico. In spite of its perfidious record and the openly professed purposes and objectives of its authors and managers, our American foreign policy directorate stubbornly refuses to recognize that the Red conspiracy is a ruthless unmoral force that cannot rest until it has conquered everybody and everything on earth.

Our determination to avoid "coming to grips" with the reality of Communist criminality has now hardened into our present official policy which is to avoid a "confrontation" with the Communists at all hazards and to continue to pay them blackmail with our money and the liberty and territory of other people. Our government now stakes the future of mankind upon the official conviction that Communism is "mellowing" and that the behavior and purposes of Nikita Khrushchev are more malleable than those of his predecessors in the Red Kremlin hierarchy. In the meantime, we concern ourselves officially lest rebellious slaves behind the Iron Curtain show less restraint than we do and take matters into their own hands as in Hungary in 1956. The New York Times, always a reliable guide through the thicket of our international "bi-partisan" foreign policy, put it this way:

> We must seek to discourage anti-Communist revolts in order to avert bloodshed and war. We must under our principles [sic] live with evil even if by doing so we help to stabilize tottering Communist regimes, as in East Germany, and perhaps even expose citadels of freedom, like West Berlin, to slow death by strangulation.[3]

The Conservative American cannot fathom the motivation of an American foreign policy that gives our official protection to the boundaries of Communist slavery (as in Cuba, East Germany and Hungary) but permits Communist invasion of the free world at any point at any time (as in South Vietnam, Tibet, Venezuela and British Guiana).

At the moment of this writing we are sending American soldiers ten thousand miles to fight Communists in South Vietnam while we are arresting Americans and Cuban exiles who attempt to fight the Communists in Cuba which is only ninety miles from the coast of Florida. In this process of continuous retreat we boast of preserving "peace" which is precisely what the Kremlin calls its eminently suc-

---

[3] August 16, 1961.

cessful tactic of "liberating" one free world country after another into Communist captivity by means of riots, subversion and mob violence, stimulated and supervised by its ubiquitous resident agents. Our State Department envisions a long protraction of this "peaceful competition" between our "open society" and the "closed society" called Communism. In what they plan to be our completely disarmed world of the future our diplomats see no reason why this competition should not go on indefinitely until the two rival systems are merged into some sort of political and economic consensus.

In the plain everyday language of the Conservative American, what our State Department is proposing is the abject surrender of our freedom and national independence. Fortunately, there is available to Congress and to the American people a scientific and thoroughly effective antidote for this poisonous policy.

Continuously, for forty years our government has retained the full-time services of an internationally renowned specialist on the subject of Communism. The advice he gives, upon request, to government officials is a classified secret but periodically J. Edgar Hoover makes public statements in the course of which he reiterates the substance of what he said to the National Convention of the American Legion at Las Vegas, Nevada, in October, 1962:

> We are at war with this sinister conspiracy [Communism]. Every Communist today must be considered our enemy wherever he may be, at home or abroad. A "soft" approach toward the menace of Communism can lead only to national disaster.

. . . .

Mr. Robert Kennedy, as Attorney General of the United States, called Mr. Hoover "my professional" on the subject of Communism. Hr. Hoover is indeed the "professional" of and for the entire United States government on that critical subject. That being so, the Conservative American wonders why the State Department has ignored Mr. Hoover's professional findings and listened instead to Dr. Walt Rostow, who has no obvious background of experience with the Communist conspiracy, and, who, for that reason, perhaps, has maintained that "peace" and a "consensus" is on the agenda of Soviet American relationships.

If a private citizen were caught dealing with a Communist agent, Mr. Hoover, as Director of the FBI, would put such citizen under continuous surveillance. How is this proper precautionary practice reconciled with our continuous, open and secret deals with the enemy at the top diplomatic levels? If, as Mr. Hoover submits, "between 70 and 80 per cent of the Soviet officials in the United States have espionage assignments," then the odds are either 7 to 3 or 8 to 2 that the Soviet diplomats who are talking to our representatives in Washington and/or at the United Nations about our disarmament and other things are Communist spies. Are the "agreements" that come out of these conferences to be accepted at face value and are we prepared to liquidate our national defenses as a result of these negotiations?

The Conservative American would like to have Mr. J. Edgar Hoover answer these questions before the United States Senate Committee on Foreign Relations and before the Senate Armed Services Committee. The Conservative American is convinced that Mr. Hoover is correct. We *are* at war with Communism. This war is the inevitable and unceasing conflict between two squarely and flatly contradictory institutions, namely, Americanism and Communism. Communism is by its profession, nature, practice and purpose an unequivocal denial of every one of the four basic supporting affirmations of Americanism.

The first basic American affirmation is the existence, power and providence of Almighty God. We made this affirmation with the first breath of the new life of our republic. In the American Declaration of Independence we proclaimed that the existence of God is a self-evident truth. We said that God exists: not as a matter of faith but as a matter of fact. This truth is the basic first cornerstone of our politically organized society. Without God, none of our legal and political institutions make sense.

Communism hits this affirmation "head-on." Communism is the activation of militant marching atheism. Every single one of its plans, purposes and postulates is predicated upon the assumption that the only acceptable omnipotence is the ruling Communist dictatorship. The slightest compromise with this assumption would cause the whole Communist apparatus to fall apart.

The second basic American affirmation is the temporal and eternal *personal* responsibility of the individual citizen. As Madison stated in the *Federalist*,[4] our entire political experiment swings upon our capacity to govern ourselves according to the moral law. It was upon this assumption that the founding fathers moved on to the third supporting pillar of our system, namely, constitutionally limited government. The only people who can afford the great luxury of a civil government strictly limited by law are those people who recognize and are willing to live by their natural, God-imposed obligations and responsibilities under the Ten Commandments. In the Pennsylvania wilderness, a

---

[4] Number 39.

hundred years before Madison was born, William Penn had declared that "those people who will not be governed by God will be ruled by tyrants." The prescient leaders, who with Madison, put the great timbers of our Constitutional structure in place, remembered that, too. There is no protection against tyranny nor for the endurance and conservation of constitutional limitation upon the power of government, except in the moral government of each man by his faith and by himself, under God.

The activated atheism called Communism sweeps away both of these American affirmations at the same time: In the Communist dispensation there are no God-given rights and no God-imposed responsibilities because there is no God but the state. Under Communism, human beings are merely in the higher order of material "things." Under such circumstances, constitutional limitations would be an insult to the ruling authorities who are the absolute owners and commanders of every person and thing under their jurisdiction.

The final basic affirmation of Americanism is the natural institution of private property which it is the primary purpose of Communism to destroy.

At every pivotal point, therefore, sparks fly and shocks reverberate when Communism confronts Americanism. The Communists have never hesitated to proclaim this generic incompatibility of their institution with ours, and the refusal of our foreign policy governors to recognize it now as clearly as they did in 1920 is inexplicable.

The Conservative American wants this state of war, which has been acknowledged by J. Edgar Hoover, to be declared and acknowledged by the Congress of the United States. Resolutions have been introduced in Congress to bring about such a declaration and the Conservative American believes that these should be revised and supported. We cannot go forward with the restoration and conservatism of our basic American resources, namely, personal liberty, constitutional government and national independence until the big Red roadblock is removed from the pathway of human freedom here and all over the world.

The Communists have blackmailed the whole course of their brutal conquest across the world with the threat of nuclear war. This criminal operation, like all successful blackmail, has been predicated upon the calculated weakness of the victim rather than the strength of the criminal who has practiced it. The victim of highway robbery may lose his money but he can keep his self-respect. The victim of blackmail loses both, not once merely but time and again interminably.

Because Stalin threatened to make a separate peace with Hitler, we gave him his "second front" in France rather than through the "soft underbelly" at the Balkans which would have shut him off from his coveted conquest of eastern Europe. When Stalin threatened to destroy President Roosevelt's dream of the United Nations, we forgot the matter of free elections and gave him a free hand with one hundred million formerly free people in more than twenty previously independent nations. Because Khrushchev threatened nuclear war, we permitted him to build the Berlin Wall and promised to protect from invasion his new Communist colony in the western hemisphere.

In the passionate pursuit of "peace" we now propose to disarm ourselves and hand over the problem of our national defense to the tender mercies of the United Nations while we engage in "trade" with our implacable Communist enemies.

Criminologists recognize that the victim of blackmail has three and only three possible courses of action against his criminal tormentor. The victim may (a) continue to pay the blackmailer, or (b) he may kill the blackmailer, or (c) he may free himself by telling the truth that he is paying the blackmailer to conceal.

For twenty years our government has been paying the Soviet blackmailer with one concession after another. It is obvious now that the extortioner will be satisfied with nothing short of the complete and unconditional surrender of our national life. To "kill" the blackmailer might or might not require a nuclear war but for those who would "rather be Red than dead," there is still the third alternative; *We can tell the truth* and the truth—now as in 1776—will make us free.

The truth is that there is no such thing as a *legitimate* Communist government anywhere on earth. The truth is that what our State Department calls the "closed societies" of Communism are iron-ringed jails from which the inmates may attempt to escape only at the risk of their lives. The truth is that conditions in these Communist jails are so horrible that hundreds of people risk and often lose their lives in attempts to escape from them. The truth is that the hundreds of millions of helpless people who are held in this monstrous Red captivity are scandalized by the calloused indifference of our government to their cruel fate as expressed in a foreign policy which is deliberately calculated to "help stabilize tottering Communist regimes, as in East Germany."

The truth is that without our positive and active help, all of these "tottering Communist regimes" would fall of their own weight within six months after our help was withdrawn.

The truth is that if we withdrew our official prohibition against an invasion of the Red Chinese mainland by the Nationalist Chinese

Army on Formosa that invasion would take place immediately, and 90 per cent of the enslaved Chinese on the mainland would join the attack against their Red Chinese jailers.

This would solve our problem in South Vietnam and Laos where the Red forces are being supplied and supervised by the Red Chinese government. The collapse of Communism in China would start a chain reaction of anti-Communist revolution which would sweep across Europe to the eastern boundary of West Germany.

The consequences of *an official proclamation of the truth about Communists and Communist governments by the government of the United States* would open the door to the destruction of Communism by its own oppressed victims without international war and without the use of American military forces.

The truth is that we are deliberately helping the Communist dictators to remain in power because the liberal–internationalist establishment which has controlled our government for thirty years wishes to use Communism as a ploy to bring about the eventual establishment of a "consensus," namely universal "Democratic Socialism" under world government.

The Conservative American knows that the cry of "peace, peace, when there is no peace" but only continuous surrender to a relentless foe in a world-wide war is sheer political hypocrisy. He realizes that little or nothing can be done about the conservation of our eroding resources of precious moral principle until we "come to grips" with Communism which is now reversing the course of western civilization and turning it into a torrent of atheistic barbarism.

The truth that made us free will restore our freedom now and lift the hearts and hopes of millions whom our present policy of retreat and surrender has doomed to perpetual slavery. Let us therefore tell the truth. The Conservative American believes that:

> We should declare the world Communist movement an outlaw in the community of civilized nations. Accordingly, we should withdraw diplomatic recognition from all Communist governments, including that of the Soviet Union, thereby serving notice on the world that we regard such governments as neither legitimate nor permanent.[5]

This will not be a signal for international nuclear war but for successful anti-Communist revolution which will melt down the Iron Curtain from the inside. This is the high road of moral principle that leads to peace with freedom for America and for mankind.

---

[5] *The Conscience of A Conservative*, by Barry Goldwater (Shepardsville, Ky.: Victor Publishing Co., 1960), p. 120.

Chapter Three

The Far Right in Action

The voice of the extreme right as presented in the first two chapters is a shrill one, full of bitter complaints about the state of the world today and certain in its knowledge of the reasons for the troubles of the United States. To those unsympathetic to the rightists, there seems to be little in modern life that pleases them, and they have been accused more than once of wanting to repeal the twentieth century.

Perhaps this is so, but it is also true that rightists have played a part in the creation of twentieth-century America. And the deeds of the right are at least as important as its motives and its rhetoric for the student who wishes to understand the movement. Hence in this chapter we will look through the eyes of several commentators at how extreme rightists go about their business of combating communism and promoting Americanism.

Houston's Superpatriots*

Willie Morris

In its campaign to save the United States from subversion, the right has taken deepest root in the southwestern states and in Southern California. Explanations for this will be touched on in the course of various articles in this book. For a case study of the many and varied activities of the extreme right

---

Harper's Magazine (October, 1961), 48–56.

in its natural habitat, one could hardly do better than take a good look at its effect upon Houston. That is what the following article does. It was written by William W. Morris, a native Texan who was editor of a weekly newspaper, the *Texas Observer*. Once editor of the student newspaper at the University of Texas, Morris was president of the American Students Association when he attended Oxford as a Rhodes Scholar. He is now chief editor of *Harper's Magazine*.

Last summer a member of the Texas House of Representatives was walking down a busy thoroughfare in Houston when suddenly he heard a booming voice proclaim, "America is a republic. It is *not* a democracy." He looked around for the source. It was a loudspeaker in a low-flying airplane, and attached to the tail of the craft was a huge streamer which cryptically advised, "Impeach Earl Warren."

It takes uncommon self-assurance, even in Texas, to make the sky your rostrum. But in Houston a battalion of salvationists have recently commandeered the heavens—and hundreds of more mundane platforms—to preach their diverse superpatriotic certitudes. In growing numbers, the citizens of that expansive country town are listening in rapt attention, believing—or fearing—that these compelling evangelists of the far right have found the definitive answer to the world's troubles. We more retiring Texans are beginning to watch in awe the rise of this prairie mecca for political messiahs—both the John Birchers and the older native sectarians as well—who may soon make eccentric Los Angeles look modest by comparison.

In this adolescent among American cities—it was twentieth in population in 1940 and is now sixth—these peddling patriots have a rich market. For the oil and chemical capital of the world is only a few years and a few miles removed from the hellfire faiths of the frontier. The strength and intensity of the superpatriotic movement owe much to a yearning after the old-style pulpit evangelism, a brooding suspicion of "intellectuals," a temperamental distrust of what the Feds are up to in Washington, a rising fear of Communist successes in a world threatened by nuclear destruction. Houston is a city of newcomers, and the newcomers are on the make: young men and women fresh from the East Texas boondocks, young professionals and technicians and industrial managers from all over the nation who are turning the swamps into scrubbed suburbias and who often are willing to take the nostrums of their bosses as their very own.

These modern patrioteers have been active in Houston for quite a while. In 1953 the *Houston Post* published a devastating series on the

Minute Women, a feminine vigilante group which competes with the
musca domestica in nuisance value. "There exists a reign of terror
among patriotic clergymen, editors, and schoolteachers here," the
Post said, "particularly those in the slightest interested in social im-
provements." From all indications, however, the fifties were nothing
more than a gestation period. As the Cold War gets colder, and particularly since the election of a reforming Democratic Administration
and the impertinences of Castro, the Houston patrioteers have got
going as never before. Of late they have been sharing their homey
wisdom with PTA's, churches and church groups, school assemblies,
plush banqueting forums, military reserve meetings, civic clubs,
professional caucuses, and neighborhood socials. Their favorite movie
dramas—the House Un-American Activities Committee's *Operation
Abolition* and the ominous film from Searcy, Arkansas, *Communism
on the Map*—have perhaps reached more people in Houston than *Gone
with the Wind.* You can hear the patrioteering folk on radio, watch them
on television, and follow their escapades in the newspapers; and they
have promoted the tape-recorded "message" into what now must be
one of the most booming businesses in the Southwest. Anyone who
has watched them at work for a spell, in fact, will begin to suspect that
the tape-recording people are behind it all. A Houston patrioteer without a tape recorder is like his pioneer grandpap without a six-shooter.

Mr. Robert Welch, the majordomo of the John Birch Society, has
named Houston and Los Angeles his two strongest cities. But his
Houston prestige is enhanced, he has explained, because "you do not
have the left-wing opposition in Houston that we have in places like
Los Angeles. . . . " This assurance did not dissuade a local disciple, who
owns a laundry and sponsors some of the more enlightening radio
shows, from hiring private detectives to protect him from the city's
subversives. In a tape-recorded talk before the Salesmanship Club in
the Rice Hotel, he said, "The John Birch Society does not see Communists under every bed because American cowards have already taken
all the room." Asked about Attorney General Kennedy's statement that
he was having the FBI check on the Birchers, he replied. "I had a member of my chapter do that [run a check] on the society and on me. Then
I told him, 'Son, it takes two to tango, so I'm going to have you checked.'
I haven't seen him since."

When Mr. Welch himself came to town at the invitation of the local
Sons of the American Revolution, he spoke before three thousand
cheering souls and a galaxy of tape recorders. After the three Houston
dailies published critical editorials on the Birch Society, the letters-to-
the-editor columns crackled in defense. "If Mr. Robert Welch is a

paranoiac," said a fairly typical missive, "then let us have more para-
noiacs in Washington instead of the eggheads who managed, in fifteen
short years, to reduce the greatest nation on the face of the earth into
an abjectly humiliated, morally weakened, almost bankrupt laughing
stock of the world. What manner of men may these be, who extended
their liberal cause to benefit the enemy?"

The patrioteers have opened a Conservative Bookstore in a new
suburban shopping center. Here such literary and philosophical guide-
posts as *The Income Tax–Root of All Evils, A Youth's Primer to the
Confederacy–What the Historians Left Out,* and *How to Plan an Anti-
Subversive Seminar* are available for purchase or browsing. A nice
cross section of Birch literature can be had there, along with the collected writings of Adam Smith, Herbert Spencer, and William F.
Buckley, Jr. Latest intelligence reports are displayed on the bulletin
board, where one finds exposed the brainwashing movies being shown
"right here in Houston"—including such films as *Inherit the Wind,
Exodus,* and *Spartacus.* In contrast, the board announces that the
Cardinal Mindszenty Foundation has seventy chapters in Houston and
may be heard each night on Station KTRH fighting for freedom. Clip-
pings of local speeches by gentlemen like J. Bracken Lee of Utah, "a
great patriot" who believes in great reforms "including repeal of the
income tax," are also on exhibit.

During this spring and summer [1961], some of America's most
dedicated oracles came to town. Kenneth Goff, pastor of an independent
Baptist church in Denver and an occasional platform speaker with
Gerald L. K. Smith, visited in June. He told his audience he had been a
member of the Communist party from 1936 to 1939. Since he broke
with the Communists, he said, his life has been in constant danger. He
slapped his artificial leg and said the Reds pushed him under a train.
"Unless the people of this country are awakened," he warned, "I give
this country less than ten years before socialism takes over completely." There are, he said, 7,000 to 8,000 Communists and fellow travelers in American churches and 1,600 in the teaching profession,
although he could not recall the names of any of them in Houston. His
visit was sponsored by several businessmen and by the Gulf Coast
United Anti-Communist League.

Dr. Billy James Hargis, founder of Christian Crusade out of Tulsa,
also a June visitor, arrived in a streamlined, air-conditioned bus with
two bedrooms, two baths, a living room, and a radio-telephone. He
stayed long enough to condemn, as the *Houston Chronicle* reported,
"Communism, liberalism, the National Council of Churches, federal

aid to education, Jack Paar, federal medical care for the aged, Ed Sullivan, the recent Kennedy–Khrushchev meeting, Eleanor Roosevelt, disarmament, Steve Allen, and the Freedom Riders." Speaking before a phalanx of tape recorders, he dismissed the brotherhood-of-man idea as "hogwash." I find most of those who criticize me are allied with those who follow the [Communist] party line," he confided.

Major Edgar C. Bundy, general chairman of the Church League of America and author of *Collectivism in the Churches*, stopped off in May. The following, he disclosed, are helping communism in the United States: the churches and church leaders, educators, newspapers, the YWCA, the American Civil Liberties Union, the White House, advisers for the Peace Corps, the Supreme Court, and thousands of Americans "who have been duped by the Communist-front organizations. . . . [J. Edgar] Hoover said the only way to combat the Communist menace in the churches is by sticking to the fundamentals of religion. I can just hear the liberals in Houston screaming at Hoover's words."

Clarence Manion, former dean of the Notre Dame law school, a member of the Birch Society council, and the Birchers' favorite to take over for Chief Justice Earl Warren after they get the latter impeached, also came to town in May, invited by the Houston Bar Association to speak at naturalization ceremonies on Law Day. "Don't tell me of the shrinking, gutless Americans—some of them in high places—I say to them, talk not to me of peace at a time like this. I am fed to the teeth with equivocations." He modestly admitted that support of him for a Supreme Court post by some Birchers was "just an academic accolade."

Dan Smooth, a news commentator, came down to keynote a July the Fourth rally. He spent a good part of his time discussing the kinship of modern liberalism with socialism and bolshevism. Asking for a restriction of federal power, he said the taxes levied by government today are used to finance "things far more harmful than King George the Third ever thought of." Smoot had an audience of forty thousand.

So it goes, this upsurge of the patrioteers in the South's largest city. How can it be explained? Why is the lushest growth in Houston rather than Memphis or Fort Worth or particularly Dallas, a town whose civic conservatism has been more abiding than Houston's?

For one thing, a militant climate of anti-intellectualism is natural in any burgeoning provincial metropolis. For want, it would seem, of better-rooted and more sophisticated wisemen, many in the town accept uncritically those forceful and self-assured preachers, company executives, insurance men, doctors, and industrial consultants as experts on public affairs and particularly on the last several decades of

American history. A typical audience of Houston patrioteers would take the word of one wealthy insurance executive on the Communist menace in preference to the combined wisdom of George Kennan, Arthur Schlesinger, Jr., Isaiah Berlin, Edmund Wilson, and Dean Rusk. The patrioteers thrive on the homespun democratic idea that a man need have no credentials to be an expert. His best equipment is a good speaking voice, knowledge of the Scriptures, and a towering dedication. It is no surprise that in the vernacular of the Houston patrioteers, intellectuals are habitually labeled "ineffectual" or "soft on Communism." A recent issue of a local patrioteering newsletter, for example, in discussing the U-2 incident and speculation on whether Powers was shot down, concluded: "Those facets we'll leave for the intellectual 'duplomats' to discuss."

Much of this distrust of the "intellectuals" has been channeled into protests against dangerous books. In 1957 a member of the school board initiated a controversy by condemning a textbook which had a preface praising the UN, a chapter entitled "It's All One World," and a passage saying the government is obligated "to promote the welfare of the people." Recently J. D. Salinger has been catching some of this provincial wrath. A prominent Houston lawyer and member of the Port Commission announced he was withdrawing his daughter from the University of Texas at the end of the semester when he learned she was required to read *Catcher in the Rye* in an English class. The aggrieved father sent copies to the governor, the chancellor of the university, and a number of state officials. The state senator from Houston threatened to read passages from the book on the senate floor to show the sort of thing they teach in Austin. The lawyer–father said Salinger used language "no sane person would use" and accused the university of "corrupting the moral fibers of our youth." He added that the novel "is not a hard-core Communist-type book, but it encourages a lessening of spiritual values which in turn leads to communism."

The executive secretary of the United Society of Methodist Laymen, Inc., who travels all over the country and who says he gets his strongest support in Houston, told a large gathering of matrons in the Briarcroft Club that American youth is being demoralized by pornographic literature in Protestant churches. "It is part of an attempt to transform the Christian faith into a sex cult and to raise your children as a generation of sex perverts," he said, speaking before a bank of twenty tape recorders. The first rule of communism is to corrupt the young, he warned. "Only one thing can stop me in this campaign," the Houston *Post* reported him as saying. "That's death itself. If it be at the hands of Communist bullets, so be it."

One civic-minded matron and Birch member in Channelview, on Houston's outskirts, discovered there was a book, *Living Biographies of Greek Philosophers,* in the school library. "Plato talks about free love and communal living and such, and that's not meant for thirteen- and fourteen-year-olds," she said. Also, Plato was a student of Socrates and "the people at that time poisoned Socrates for the ideas he was spreading," she remembered. "The school library must be cleaned out. I haven't been in it, but they have many books, and some bad ones are bound to slip through." Happily, at the next meeting of the district school board, the trustees staved off attempts at censorship, refused to have the meeting tape-recorded, and reported that the superintendent himself was compiling a study of library books.

A second major source of the patrioteers' fervor is the fearsome evangelical fundamentalism which is native to the East Texas Bible Belt and funnels into metropolitan Houston. The literature of the superpatriots bristles with indictments of "liberal theology" and seeks a return to strict fundamentalist doctrine. In its brimming emotionalism, a Houston anti-Communist rally is much like a religious tent revival. The rhetoric is often Biblical; the stress is on a dedication of Christian souls to ferret out the Reds at home and abroad; the "lost" are those duped by FDR and the Communists, who have departed from the simple earthy faith of their fathers to take up such Kremlin-oriented schemes as urban renewal, aid to depressed areas, and labor unions. To the free-wheeling Houston evangelists, if the National Council of Churches is not an adjunct of the Kremlin, it is most assuredly in active radio contact.

The Belfort Baptist Church was not content this year to withdraw from one convention, it withdrew from three: the Union Baptist Association, the Baptist General Convention of Texas, and the Southern Baptist Convention. The preacher commented: "Only the old is good, but this new or neo-orthodoxy is of the devil." A local Methodist minister has been making the rounds of other churches, civic clubs, and military units with a pat sermon entitled "Who Else Serves Communism?" "Those who serve communism," he declares, "are not just those in Moscow, the fellow travelers, and dupes, but also those who claim to believe in God, and by their lives endorse the atheistic view of communism."

But the fundamentalist sects have not been alone in rejecting the social gospel. There have been similar rumblings, for instance, from the Episcopal church that serves River Oaks, the most exclusive residential area in the city. A group of ultra-conservative businessmen has just organized an "Association for Christian Schools" with the purpose of advancing "the cause of Christian education." One of the names affixed to the explanatory letter was one T. Robert Ingram, rector of another Episcopal church, St. Thomas, in one of the city's newer suburbs. As an Episcopalian, Ingram holds an undisputed lead as High Priest of the Houston patrioteers. His picture adorns a wall of the Conservative Bookstore, and from all one can gather he believes the world has been drifting steadily toward bolshevism since Genesis 1:1. Ingram has edited a pamphlet entitled *Essays on Segregation*, billed as "a collection of writings by six Episcopalian clergymen, one of them a bishop, exploring the Christian foundations for the racial settlement in the South called segregation, and exposing 'integration' as an attack on mankind's greatest treasure, faith in Jesus Christ." In a typical sermon, he rather curiously linked "this matter of mental health" with the ominous power by which "labor unions have marched to virtual control of all governments in the United States."

In this atmosphere, it was no surprise that when President Kennedy appeared before the Houston ministers in his dramatic confrontation of the religious issue last autumn, the first question asked him concerned, not separation of church and state, but the right-to-work laws.

Under this steady crossfire from fellow gentlemen of the cloth, a number of Protestant leaders have fought back. Bishop James A. Pike of California came to town and charged that an Episcopal layman in Houston had "smeared" him as a Communist and that the Houston Minute Women "had used pamphlets and pressured university officials" in an unsuccessful attempt to keep him from speaking at Rice last year. The Association of Churches of Greater Houston has established a committee to combat charges of infiltration. "A lot of good men have been maligned and made victims of virtual character assassination by people coming in and making charges of communism," said the president, a Presbyterian minister. "The committee is the result of our just getting fed up about being charged with everything from communism to sex disorders."

By all odds the most effective single agency in uniting fervent evangelism with thundering conservatism in Houston has been a national organization called the Christian Anti-Communism Crusade. Going about their work with all the primitive vigor of an orgiastic sunrise revival, the Crusaders spoke 300 times in Houston in 1960 to more than 60,000 people in churches, schools, clubs, and business groups.

The guiding light behind the Crusade nationally is a former

Australian medical doctor named Fred C. Schwarz; it is his admiring disciple, W. P. Strube, Jr., who leads the fight in Houston. Strube's academic grounding was in Naval ROTC at two West Coast universities, and he is now president of an insurance company. He modestly concedes in one of his many pocket-sized pamphlets that he is "one of America's leading authorities" on the subject of "the Communists' tactics in the Cold War." According to Strube, the testimony of his tutor, Dr. Schwarz, before the House Un-American Activities Committee "had a wider circulation in this country than any document except possibly the Bill of Rights, the Declaration of Independence, and the Constitution." When he first heard Schwarz in 1952, "I shivered and shook for ten minutes, took a towel of apathy, and went about my way." Later, when he found the Australian to be "the most dedicated man I ever knew," he joined the Crusade in earnest and is now vice-president.

"Why am I doing it?" Strube says. "I have two reasons. I have two beautiful children, whom I love very much."

Strube is a fearsome platform orator, often hypnotic in effect. By his own count he spoke against communism 150 times in 1958, 300 times in 1959, and about 400 times in 1960. The Crusade, in addition, distributes pamphlets and books by the gross, as well, of course, as tape recordings (such as "Why Do Millionaires, Ministers of Religion, and College Professors Become Communists" and "Insurance Against Communism"). Strube's office is equipped with nine portable tape recorders tended by technicians taping new and old talks by Strube and his associates, along with three-giant tape-reproducing machines.

In one of Strube's early manuals, a crude mimeographed affair as compared to the slick literature he circulates today, he sounded a clarion which seemed to suggest that he would have been happier with a saber and a commission from J. E. B. Stuart. "Carrying on the lessons from the militia in wartimes as it existed in the United States from 1776 until nearly the outbreak of World War II," he wrote, "these political guerrilla bands must be tightly organized. Few in numbers, but mighty in Spirit could well serve as a Modus Operandi." He advised: "If you become depressed, write us for suggestions on how to rehabilitate your group. . . . By using tape recordings, the experts can be taken into homes, schools, Sunday schools, classes, etc. . . . We must have fast and mass dissemination of the information if we are to preserve our freedom."

Strube's prose sometimes reads like a military dispatch from Richard Coeur de Lion: "Take first the helmet of Salvation, then the breastplate of righteousness, gird your loins with the truth, prepare your feet for the propagation of the Gospel, which will set men free.

Take the shield of faith and the sword of the Spirit, which is the Word of God, and move forward into battle. . . . "

The Crusade's Teens Against Communism Clubs have been well received. At Jesse H. Jones High School, for instance, students attended weekly Thursday night anti-communism programs sponsored by the teen clubs themselves. Films from Harding College in Searcy, Arkansas (a kind of war college for the patrioteers of the area and perhaps of the whole nation) were shown, along with *Operation Abolition.* At one night's program, with eight hundred in attendance, the supervisor of history, economics, and civics courses in Houston's secondary schools spoke, and said the program was filled with "fine things." Strube delivered one of his basic diatribes, and a standard Crusade speaker who is guidance director in a local high school said Comminists were "very successful" in inciting the San Francisco student riots and that they were trying to make U.S. youth "decadent and immoral." He warned that the Reds are interested "in getting filthy literature in your hands. They definitely are."

Last spring Strube served as general director of a typical Crusade-originated Freedom Forum in Houston's Shamrock-Hilton hotel. He advertised the event in his newsletter:

> We trust that as the Lord challenges your heart to this missionary opportunity you will become a salesman, a prayer warrior, and a supporter of the effort. We trust that as you give your financial assistance to this cause, you will do so not grudgingly or of necessity, for the Lord loveth a cheerful giver.[1] Marx said, "Workers of the world unite, you have nothing to lose but your chains." History has proven this to be a lie. We say instead, "Americans of Houston UNITE, your most precious possession is endangered, your FREEDOM." . . .
>
> Tape Recorders—"Do It Yourself" facilities will be available for 25 recorders. 1,800 ft. blank tape, $2. "Let Us Do It"—Two Speeches on 1,800 ft. tape, $5.

There were full houses on each of the four Saturdays in the Emerald Room of the Shamrock-Hilton, and some two thousand additional townsfolk watched the doings in an adjoining room on closed-circuit television. Films, tape recordings, and lectures were featured on the programs, which began at 9:30 A.M. and lasted until late into the night.

Schwarz, the Crusade president and one of the lecturers, said everything is a weapon in the Cold War, including art, religion, language,

---

[1] Philip Horton, in *The Reporter* (July 20, 1961), said that gross receipts of the Crusade, a tax-free organization, were $63,000 in 1957, $380,000 in 1960, and estimated at one million dollars for 1961.

and diplomacy. When the Russian ballet comes to America and charms an audience, it is a victory for the Russians. The Reds are running ahead of their schedule to take over the United States by 1973. Pointing at the businessmen and junior executives assembled in the plush hall, Schwarz said, "You are the most stupid segment of the American people. Comparing your success with Communist achievements, the only possible prediction is that you won't have any businesses left in the next ten or fifteen years." Other experts included two former FBI men, an Army sergeant from San Antonio, and an industrial consultant from Kansas City.

But the holiest temple of the patrioteers has its roots even deeper in Houston than the Crusade. This is the Berachah Church, one of the most impressive new religious phenomena in the whole country. The faithful may come every day of the week except Saturdays, and three times on Sundays, for scriptural sanction. Berachah Church is "nondemoninational," dispensing the old rural fundamentalism close to the hearts of the Houston immigrants not long removed from the piney woods and swamp bottoms, but with a sharp suburban cut. As its pastor explains, "Fundamentalism has been misdefined in this country. For a generation it has been associated with frothing at the mouth and rolling in the aisles. Actually, fundamentalism is real conservatism in theology."

The sign in front of the huge streamlined temple reads: "They Assembled Themselves in the Valley of Berachah for There They Blessed the Lord." Here in a wealthy new suburban area in southwest Houston, disgruntled members of other congregations have been assembling in growing numbers. Two years ago the church was housed in a renovated Quonset hut in a somewhat shabbier precinct. Today, although the foam-rubber seats in its massive auditorium will take care of one thousand, and although there is a labyrinth of rooms built outward from it, the church is overflowing every service and the Sunday school is unable to accommodate another child. Now Berachah is expanding again with another thousand seats and additional rooms in the offing.

The tape-recording room will have to be enlarged also. Located just off the main auditorium, it will only handle three dozen machines at present, and that is not enough. Members of the congregation bring their own recorders, plug them in private outlets, and watch. There is also a "tape ministry" in Berachah Church; more than twenty recordings are made of each sermon and dispatched with zeal to all parts of the world. The pastor is well known, it is said, "for not uttering a word without a microphone in front of him."

How can Berachah's growth be explained? "Because people are starved for the word of God as it was written," a secretary said, "and not as it's being preached in some of these pulpits."

As the Berachah brethren read it, the word of God might be interpreted in its political content to be only slightly to the left of King Alfred. The pastor, Colonel Bob Thieme, is a Phi Beta Kappa graduate of the University of Arizona who had to give up a Rhodes scholarship to serve in the Army in World War II. He is now active in the Air Force reserve and is an expert pistol marksman. After the war he graduated from fundamentalist Dallas Theological Seminary. Thieme, who says five thousand people come through his church during an average week, has orated at Christian Anti-Communism Crusade functions; the Birch Society, in his opinion, "appears to be doing a very fine job." Nine times out of ten, he says, folks who are conservative about the scriptures will be conservative politically. He interprets the stanch ultra-conservatism of Houston with stark simplicity: "It's because of a wide dissemination of Bible-teaching in this area."

The role of Houston's officialdom during the rise of the patrioteers has been ambiguous. Tolerant and quiescent, perhaps through caution, the generally conservative fathers have avoided taking a stand on the superpatriots' issue-mongering. It was no surprise this July that when the Texas American Legion decided to ask Congress to investigate both the State Department and the Supreme Court, they were convening in Houston when they did it. The climate there is favorable —though certainly not every city official is a Bircher or a Minute Woman. Quite the contrary: recent mayors have been liberal or moderately so; city politics is free-wheeling and open.

The Houston school board, however, regularly sallies forth on ideological tangents congenial to the patrioteers. So much so that the board itself has become one of the most avidly discussed topics in town, and its televised sessions are sometimes called the "Monday night fights." The school board's politically colored actions began in the fifties when anti-UNESCO candidates ran in the elections; "Save the Schools from Socialism" was a favorite rallying cry; and textbooks were expurgated for sundry reasons. Liberal–conservative margins were often close, but there was allegedly a time when a majority of the members were either Minute Women or husbands of Minute Women. The present president of the board is a member of the DAR and a winner of the Houston Sons of the Revolution's award for her "continuing battle against socialistic liberalism in modern education." She has also been victorious in rejecting federal funds for milk for school children.

It would be difficult, in. fact, to distinguish some of the recent actions of the board from the practical dictums of a Birch study cell. For example, this summer the local chapter of the American Civil Liberties Union wanted to rent one of the school auditoriums for a talk by its national executive secretary, Patrick Malin. But the board members, alert to all threats, promptly passed a motion (with one dissenting vote cast by Mrs. Charles E. White, a Negro and the sole liberal on the board) denying auditorium facilities to any organization or persons whose thinking "was not in keeping with that of Houstonians." This disposed of, the board later announced that two loyalty oaths would be required for future rentals: one by a representative of the applying group and another by the proposed speaker. "We don't want any Communist speakers or Communist group meetings in our public schools," the president said.

Again the board bestirred itself when a lady named Margaret Bleil, who had thirty years' teaching experience, was recommended for a higher position by both her school principal and the city superintendent. Unfortunately, she had been president of the Houston Teachers' Association seven years ago when that organization had invited the National Education Association to do a study of the Houston schools. The NEA made a rather unfavorable report. Although Mrs. Bleil as president of the teachers' organization had not cast a vote when the invitation was made, her promotion was not approved; as the vice-chairman of the board explained later, "Someone as controversial as that should not be promoted."

Yet another case involved a young history teacher named Kenneth Parker. A local Minute Woman had heard that Parker had dropped a few controversial comments in class. In order to check for herself, she invited him to her home. She played a tape recording of a patrioteering speech and quizzed Parker on his opinions. Since she was not satisfied, she consulted her friend, the school-board president, who instituted a more formal check on the teacher. Meanwhile, the civic-minded Minute Woman reportedly received special reports from adults who came into Parker's classes and took notes. After a prolonged controversy, he resigned, affirming in exasperation that he was a Christian, a John Fitzgerald Kennedy Democrat, and an active Democratic precinct worker. The Minute Woman and her spouse commented that his departure was a good thing "because of his reluctance to tell us he was a Christian and the ultra-liberal views he expounded in the classroom." The school board at first accepted his resignation; later he was merely suspended temporarily, then transferred to another high school and placed on "day-to-day" probation. Young Parker, who has since had a more lucrative teaching job offered in New York, was not a good sport about it; he said his encounter with the Minute Woman was the beginning of an "eleven-month organized, anonymous plot to humiliate, embarrass, and harass me."

Houston is "the last stronghold and concentrated seat of rugged individualism," says the director of city planning, and he goes back to the early ranch economy of the area to help explain it. On this rugged tradition has been superimposed the gloss of first- and second-generation wealth.

"Abolish the Income Tax"—that perennial slogan of the wealthy right—is a magnet for new patrioteers. As a local realtor likes to say in describing one of the inveterate contributors, "He'd rather get a part of the income tax abolished than be visited every night of the year by six sixteen-year-old virgins."

When H. L. Hunt, the Dallas billionaire, decided last spring to break a long public silence and come to Houston for some speech-making, it was like the entry of a saintly old warrior knight into a camp of medieval barons. "The country is so far gone," advised the man who subsidizes more political proselytizing than just about any-one else in the nation and who advocated in his novel, *Alpaca*, that the right to vote be based on wealth, "that I am willing to do anything I can to dispel the apathy of the people." He said, among other things: Calvin Coolidge was the last president he approved; 2 per cent of the American people are Reds, 2 per cent active patriots, 18 per cent Red sympathizers or dupes, and the remaining 78 per cent "dormand"; the eleven billion dollars a year which business spends on advertising should be used to promote patriotic themes. At a press conference, his daughters sang new words to songs which expressed their father's views, such as this stanza to the tune of "School Days":

> Listen to what our Popsy says,
> Don't give an inch to any Red . . . .

Although there are notable exceptions, rare indeed is the Houston magnate of new money who would not stand squarely with Hunt and Cal Coolidge in the political spectrum, several degrees to the right of the late Robert A. Taft. So much of the big Houston money was made overnight by digging a hole in the ground, or passed along intact from quick-rich fathers, that as one Houstonian explains it, "They've sud-denly come into a lot of money, and they're afraid the government's going to take it away from them." Equally exasperated, large numbers of the more moderately rich have concluded that they are "working for someone else." They are looking for sweeping answers, and among the Houston patrioteers, sweeping answers are part of the business.

Four years or so ago, when the liberal movement in Texas began to cast a dark shadow across the city, a number of the Houston oil, gas, insurance, and utilities companies—usually the home-based ones —began importing firebrand speakers of the George Roberts type. (George Roberts, a former college teacher of hazy academic background, was hired as "industrial consultant" by several large Houston firms which felt that their employees needed their politics straightened out. He was also signed up to give five required lectures to all history, civics, and economics teachers in the Houston system.) Seminars for company executives became a standard practice. Freedom-In-Action, a semi-secret political organization which is the brainchild of Houston's own Elwood Fouts, an active Liberty Leaguer in the 'thirties, moved into the breach. For the city's growing class of junior executives, political-action movements of the conservative stripe have become just another part of getting ahead.

Many good ladies of leisure have likewise contributed to the rise of the patrioteers—housewives in Tanglewood and in the cloistered piney woods around Memorial Drive as well as in the newer and slightly less elite suburbs. "Their husbands are on the way up," one slightly cynical matron says, "and they suddenly become aware of this income-tax business." They are usually more vocal and more active in letter writing and the busier types of nagging agitation than the patrioteer male of the species.

The Houston Junior Chamber of Commerce, which sometimes likes to call itself the largest Jaycee organization in the world, has provided a central forum for the patrioteers, and serves as a fairly reliable gauge of the raging dissastisfactions of the younger business set. A recent president, William Hollis, is a full-time, salaried organizer for the political movement, Freedom-In-Action. Jaycee banquets have been well stocked with speakers like Strube and Fouts. At a recent Jaycee-sponsored political rally, one of the more vociferous local patrioteers—a candidate for Congress on the far-right Constitutional party ticket who has challenged Lyndon Johnson to fist fights in his speeches—was introduced as the Houston Jaycees' "Man of the Year." The organization has also recently given an "Americanism" award to Fouts, which is at least tantamount to tacit approval of his organization's perfervid opposition to social security, unemployment compensation, foreign aid, the United Nations, and all the classic bugaboos of the patrioteers.

The contrast which Houston presents in relation to Dallas these days is striking. Big D, only 240 miles away, has been a traditional center of conservatism in the Southwest. It most assuredly has never been without what George Fuermann, in his excellent Texas study, *Reluctant Empire*, calls "a minority of fanatical nationalists." Anti-Semitism has never been a flaming issue in Houston as it has sometimes been in Dallas, and art exhibitions have never been expunged in Houston with such fine relish. Dallas conservatism, however, is more abiding. Houston could be a liberal city at some point in the future, as it has threatened to be on occasion in the past; but it will probably take a revolution for Dallas ever again to vote Democratic. Dallas conservatism, withal, is more sophisticated, just as the city itself. But Houston, says Hubert Mewhinney of the *Houston Post*, is a whiskey and trombone town.

Being more openly and ardently democratic, Houston is a city of taut ideological extremes. It remains the center of economic liberalism in Texas. It is a growing industrial city, and the clash between organized labor and management produces greater friction. The Dallas delegation to the state's lower house is conservative to the man. The Houston delegation includes two liberals, a moderate, and five conservatives. The Dallas conservatives, however, are not patrioteers; Houston's are.

The political leadership of the liberals in Houston is undoubtedly more liberal than anywhere else in the state. Correspondingly, the conservative leadership is more conservative. The middle ground has dwindled. In the recent seventy-man first primary to fill Lyndon Johnson's place in the Senate, it is significant that the candidates who finished one-two in the city were the most conservative and the most liberal in the race. Amid this growing polarization of political thought, the patrioteers have energetically interjected their rough-hewn idea that a man is either a Communist dupe or he isn't.

The active political arm of the patrioteers is Freedom-In-Action, a national but Houston-based organization which has never been wanting in appropriations to get through a difficult winter. It channels large sums of money into elections, lines up strength at the precinct level, and conducts programs on the heartier techniques of political infighting. Robert Welch listed FIA as one of the organizations his followers should support, and there is a great overlap in Houston membership. Although it is a semi-secret society, FIA is undoubtedly at its peak strength in Houston. It maintains a selective recruitment policy, and its members must sign a written pledge to guarantee them, as its literature says, "free from the intent of subversion," and to prevent "being captured and taken over by subversives." The society's textbook is secret, and a Texas journalist kicked up a minor storm two years ago when he obtained a copy and published some of its juicier passages. The society's purposes are to stamp out "the poison of communism whether labeled as liberalism, socialism, welfare statism, or communism."

In 1957 FIA produced a movie drama direct from the Boris Karloff tradition. A politically apathetic doctor falls asleep and has a nightmare; doctors are socialized, farmers await production orders from Washington, gasoline is rationed, the government has taken over the schools. He wakes up, FIA goes to work on the harried fellow, and he wins his precinct convention from the Communists. "This will scare them a little," the producer said. It was a Houston story if there ever was one.

Among Houstonians who are suspicious of superpatriotic civic work, the erratic gyrations of their vituperative and well-heeled antagonists is very frustrating. It is more difficult to carry out a hardheaded exchange with a Bircher, an FIA member, or Christian Anti-Communism Crusader than it is to induce a Soviet youth leader to debate the bourgeois merits of civil liberties.

The brooding provincial fears over a world not clearly understood, the rampant fundamentalism, the temperamental wealth, the passionate organizational work—such are the ingredients that help explain the Houston phenomenon. A Houston manufacturer who is deeply concerned with the current rise of the patrioteers perhaps is taking too dark a view, but he expresses an opinion which is shared by many: "All of our institutions have failed us when this sort of thing can happen in an American city. Maybe if they really understood what democracy is, they'd buy it."

Carnival of Hate*

Stan Twardy

A very common activity of the extreme right is the "school" or "convention," where for two or three days those who want to inform themselves about the communist menace gather to listen to speakers, see films, buy books,

---

The Progressive (October, 1963), 24–26.

talk to one another and reaffirm their faith that America needs salvation but can be saved. Boston, for example, has its annual New England Rally for God, Family & Country, and Fred C. Schwarz' Christian Anti-Communism Crusade consists mainly of a series of such "schools" held at various places throughout the United States. Tuition (admission) for those events varies— the Boston affair costs $5, a Schwarz school $20—but there is money enough to be made from them, and Schwarz has often been accused of "patriotism for profit," a charge he vigorously denies. The following article describes one man's reaction to such an event, in this case the fifth annual convention of the Christian Crusade Against Communism. The author, Stan Twardy, is the managing editor of the *Oklahoma Courier*, a Catholic newspaper.

For three days recently, the citizens of Oklahoma were treated to a bizarre performance by the leadership of America's religious, political, social, and economic right-wing extremists. The plush Skirvin Hotel in Oklahoma City served as headquarters for the fifth annual convention of the self-styled Christian Crusade against Communism, which is headed by Tulsa's tubby evangelist Billy James Hargis.

The cast of characters included such bright stars in the extremist firmament as Robert Welch, founder and director of the John Birch Society; former Army Major General Edwin A. Walker, who specializes in accusing the nation's highest officials of "treason"; and former Major George Racey Jordan, a wizard of Alice-in-Wonderland economics. Revivalist evangelist Billy James Hargis and the one-time preacher Dr. Charles Poling were on hand to expose "apostasy" among the American clergy, especially those in what was characterized as the "Communist-dominated" National Council of Churches.

The right-wing extremists came to Oklahoma because the Southwest today is more receptive to their ideas than is almost any other part of the country, with the possible exception of California and a few states of the Deep South. The "Crusaders" offered the most representative cross section of what former Vice President Richard Nixon recently described as "nuts and kooks," in American political life. The spectrum of right-wing extremism they represented includes an estimated two thousand independent groupings, which extend their influence over some ten million Americans, or so they claimed.

My exposure to the crowd at the "Crusade" confirmed my notion that the extremist appeal is clearly succeeding with people who find the complexities of modern life and the dangers of the nuclear age too fearful and frustrating to live with. They are genuinely alarmed by real and imaginary threats to America and they see the Kennedy

Administration's failure to get rid of Castro as "proof" that the United States is "soft on Communism." I came away from the convention with the conviction that their concern, frustration, and their fear of a Communist take-over of the United States, which they are assured by their leaders is now being engineered by traitors in the highest levels of government, are shamelessly exploited by profiteers, hucksters of hate, and political charlatans.

I left the proceedings convinced that the "Crusade" had unleashed a flood of hatred and suspicion whose corroding effect on society can be regarded only as a major triumph for Communism. It was the most vicious mass assault on the President and former presidents, the Congress of the United States, the U.S. Supreme Court, the American press, and civic, religious, and educational institutions ever made in this part of the country. It seemed clear to me that the extremists were attempting to pave the way for ruthless action designed to uproot what they regard as "treason" in our midst without bothering with such niceties as facts or due process of law.

With the John Birch Society clearly emerging as a unifying force among right-wing extremists, I welcomed the opportunity to take a close look at many genuine specimens of Birchers, including their leader, Robert Welch, the avuncular one-time candy manufacturer and salesman. It was Welch who received the most thunderous ovation of the "Crusade." The mere mention of his name brought many "Crusaders" to the verge of hysteria. Welch had high praise for all the "patriotic" organizations, but he left an unmistakable impression that of all the brands of anti-Communism, his was the best.

Welch delivered a dull, rambling two-hour speech on the evils of government. In awkward, bumbling fashion, he tried hard to hammer home to the audience his conviction that "all governments are stupid" and that the United States government, in addition to being sillier than others, is thoroughly infiltrated by Communists and their sympathizers. Peppered with poisonous comments about the Kennedys, the Eisenhowers, and the Trumans, Welch's speech stressed that there is no integrity or patriotism left in Washington, and that American freedom is being strangled by a bungling and treacherous officialdom. He specifically indicted the Department of State as a hotbed of treason.

Welch carefully instructed the audience that as Christians they should have no scruples about exterminating Communists, because "if they are truly Communists, they cannot be thought of as human beings." How Welch plans to oppose the external threat of Communism is not clear, since he regards NATO as a farce and has little use for the free world's military apparatus, which he seems to regard as only another extension of useless, bureaucratic, and autocratic government. Throughout his speech Welch kept fumbling in his pockets for the carefully-numbered anecdotes he uses to illustrate his set speech. His cards were obviously mixed-up and some apparently were lost, because several times he started to repeat the same anecdote, caught himself, and apologized. When, after emptying all his pockets on the rostrum, he still could not find the proper cards, Welch frankly admitted, in the understatement of the day, "The reason that I seem so confused is that I am confused."

Welch's followers circulated constantly throughout the convention distributing literature and button-holing prospective members. They pounded persistently at one point: Communism is winning in the world today because the Reds have already taken over the American press, churches, schools, unions, Congress, and the White House.

Only the degree of subservience to Communism and duplicity of former Presidents Roosevelt, Truman, and Eisenhower, and now John F. Kennedy could be open to argument, the Birch salesmen asserted. The Communist Party membership of former Secretary of State John Foster Dulles and his brother Allen, and the Communist infiltration of the State Department and Central Intelligence Agency, were affirmed repeatedly as "revealed truth."

The Birch Society, it became clear, still regards the impeachment of Chief Justice Earl Warren as its major goal, even though some rightists, including evangelist host Hargis, readily admit that their prospects are not very bright at the moment. Hargis emphasized, however, that the campaign should be continued "to scare the living daylight out of Warren."

A corpulent lady with whom Welch spoke at length after the meeting, and who later boasted of close friendship with him, told me with great assurance that Welch has discovered "new evidence" that Dr. Martin Luther King, Jr., is trying to establish a Negro Communist Soviet Republic in the Deep South.

Welch's mumbling performance was in sharp contrast to the pitch made by the prime example of the hell-and-brimstone school of right-wing showmen, retired Major General Edwin A. Walker, who even more than Welch and Hargis seemed to dominate the Oklahoma convention. A tense, twitching performer on the platform, who would obviously be much more at home in military command where he achieved a distinguished record, the General seemed driven by a compulsion to strike out at every institution and personality in American life that he held responsible for our country's failures—failures based on the nation's refusal to accept his curious interpretation of domestic and world politics.

Walker's anti-Communism tirade at the convention was directed primarily against what he described as "the contemptuous Kennedy brothers and sadistic Harvard associates, who are the temporary administrators, but not the government of the United States." Next on his hate parade are "niggers, for whom the best thing, for their own good, is to be separated."

Walker professed to see Harvard as an assembly-line factory grinding out intellectual American Communists whom the Kennedys are promptly pushing into positions of power as an "unelected" government. After "Kennedys and niggers," the greatest menace to America, Walker affirmed, is Walter W. Rostow, a high-ranking policy planner in the State Department. "I reserve the right to call him a traitor before I call him a Communist," the former general shouted to the cheering convention audience.

The general lashed out in the same breath against Fidel Castro, Dwight D. Eisenhower, and John F. Kennedy. "Any idiot can be president. Only give him a brother. Look at Raul, Milton, and Bobby," he said. The audience went wild. "The Supreme Court," Walker said, "is a tool of Communistic and atheistic conspiracy to destroy America." The hall shook with cheers.

General Walker showed some compassion in discussing Congress. "These turncoats," he said, "deserve your pity." The military establishment, he charged, is being dismantled, rendered ineffective, and prostituted by being used to invade sovereign states of the Union in attempts to enforce imaginary rights of Negroes to attend all-white schools.

Another great menace to America, Walker assured the Crusaders, are psychiatrists, for whom he reserves much of his virulence. Referring to the doctor who questioned Walker's own mental stability, and sent him to a mental hospital, the general shouted angrily, "This man's father was born in Russia, and you know what that means." Walker also charged that military psychiatrists are making heroes out of beatniks, undermining military discipline, and restricting "patriotic activities" of servicemen. As a bulwark against treason and psychiatrists, the former soldier recommended "hard-hitting brainwashing. I would call it a mental massage."

Some leaders of ultra-conservatism were obviously uncomfortable about the anti-Negro emphasis in Walker's outbursts, about his suggestion that four presidents of the United States were Communists, and his often incoherent ranting, but they nevertheless regard him as one of the best drawing cards on the right-wing circuit, a surefire attraction guaranteed to draw large audiences.

The performance in Oklahoma City was not without its political overtones. A lady with a sign, "Walker for President, He Is Our Honest Abe," was clearly let down when newscaster Fulton Lewis, Jr., asked all the conservatives to rally behind Senator Barry Goldwater for President. Lewis' speech and his question-and-answer period had little to do with Christian crusading. It was a political rally for Goldwater, and the audience loved it.

Out of the three days of oratory emerged a consensus among the "Crusaders" that the United States should break diplomatic relations with the Soviet Union and her satellites, expel the United Nations from the United States and Castro from Cuba, and consider showering the Soviet Union and Communist China with nuclear and hydrogen bombs.

On the level of economic and social philosophy the most insistent demands were for the abolition of the income tax, Social Security, the National Labor Relations Board, the Federal Reserve System, the Rural Electrification Administration, the "mental health racket," Federal aid to housing, and the Department of Agriculture with all its programs for "regimenting" farmers.

One of the chief masterminds of this rightist economic program turned out to be former Major George Racey Jordan, a publicity agent for several California gold mines. He advocated abolition of foreign aid, using the funds instead to purchase American-mined gold at $90 to $100 an ounce instead of the present $35. To ensure prosperity for American manufacturers, he would simply close the U.S. market to foreign goods, although he did not say how he would induce "Communistic and atheistic foreigners" to purchase American exports.

The economic theories of the former major kept the audience in raptured suspense. Jordan told how he single-handedly tried to prevent the Russians from robbing the United States blind during World War II. He related that on orders from "traitors in Washington" he delivered to Russia uranium with which the Soviets built their first atom bomb, and engravers' plates from which the Soviets could print their own dollars for the purchase of American goods. The audience sat spellbound.

With his guests increasingly dominating the show and competitively recruiting members from among his "Crusaders," Dr. Hargis had to be satisfied with the financial contributions he was able to extract from the audience. Pleading "for God and America," he told his listeners that "massive blood" was the alternative to financial support of his "Crusade." Instead of the $1,250,000 needed, he said, the

"Crusade" was barely getting by on $720,000 a year.

One of the more dominant themes of the "Crusade" was the charge that the vast majority of Protestant churches in the United States have become dupes and willing agents of Communism. Evangelist Hargis and former preacher Poling heaped scorn and hatred on the National Council of Churches as the arm of Communist conspiracy in America. They applied the Communist label freely to all member churches, claiming that their "apostate clergymen" now "desecrate one hundred thousand holy temples in the U.S.A. with idle talk and false doctrine."

My first-hand exposure to the extreme right in action was a profoundly disturbing experience. It reminded me of what J. Edgar Hoover had said of the futility of the whole extremist movement: "These individuals concentrate on the negative rather than on the positive. They are merely against Communism without being for any positive measures to eliminate the social, political, and economic frictions which the Communists are so adroit at exploiting. These persons would do well to recall a recent lesson from history. Both Hitler and Mussolini were against Communism. However, it was by what they stood for, not against, that history has judged them."

The Christian Crusade against Communism, despite the religious theme injected by the revivalist preachers, was clearly neither Christian nor a crusade against Communism. It struck me as a gigantic fraud, exploiting genuine patriotism and deep-rooted religious feelings and prejudices for purposes which had little to do with advancing Christianity or opposing Communism.

Water Moccasin*

G. B. Leonard

The issues that concern the far right were outlined in the preceding sections of this book, and the impression may have been given that its members spend all their time in generalized worrying about the vague menace of communism. Nothing could be farther from the truth. The rightist concerns himself deeply about dozens of specific issues, and he is ever ready to agitate via letters,

---

*From "What is an Extremist?," *Look* (October 20, 1964), 34–36.

petitions, telegrams and phone calls against creeping communism and for the maintenance of American sovereignty and independence. To the outsider this agitation sometimes seems grossly inappropriate to the situation at hand. Such was the case with Exercise Water Moccasin III, a routine Army maneuver which the rightists managed to blow up into an invasion of the United States, and which had to be partially curtailed because of their outcries.

. . . Exercise Water Moccasin III was to be one of a series of realistic U.S. Army field operations. Its purpose: to train our soldiers to cope with the kind of guerrilla warfare favored by Communist forces, notably in Vietnam. The time and place: March, 1963, Fort Stewart, Georgia, and the surrounding twenty-five hundred square miles. Many U.S. soldiers were to be involved, but the training was designed primarily for four hundred U.S. officers who had just graduated from a six-week counterguerrilla-warfare school. Also to participate were one hundred twenty-four officers from cooperating foreign nations, who had attended the school.

In the exercise, an "enemy" band (the Aggressors), played by U.S. instructors and soldiers, would launch a guerrilla attack on a "small country friendly to the United States" called "Claxtonia." This "country," named after the town of Claxton, Georgia, was actually Fort Stewart and environs. The Aggressors would try, by infiltration, propaganda and simulated raids, to overcome Claxtonia. Since civilians generally get mixed up in actual guerrilla attacks, the Army planned to ask local citizens to participate if they wished. The Georgians around Fort Stewart had played their part in previous exercises and felt a certain pride about their role in strengthening U.S. prowess.

Meanwhile, a counterguerrilla force, also simulated by U.S. officers and men, would be rushed to the mock country to seek out and stop the Aggressors. Thus, American officers, many of them on their way to Vietnam, would get training both in guerrilla and antiguerrilla warfare. With world conditions what they are, this might qualify as rather fruitful "anti-Communist" activity. That is not how the extremists saw it.

Just who started the wild rumors that finally crippled Exercise Water Moccasin III is hard to say. But one of the first to turn in a false alarm was the Texas Voters for Enforcing the Constitution. In its January, 1963, letter, reprinted by the Keep America Committee, the organization came up with this interpretation of Exercise Water Moccasin III:

> This week we have reports from the East and West Coast that the UNITED NATIONS—(COMMUNIST CONTROLLED—the Commander-in-Chief of the UN Security Council and all UN Military, Naval and Air forces is PERPETUALLY A COMMUNIST—SO FAR ALWAYS A RUSSIAN GENERAL)—is staging vast NATO exercises. . . . We understand that—
>
> U.S. ARMY CIVILIAN AGENTS ARE ATTEMPTING TO LEASE 2,500 SQUARE MILES OF EASTERN GEORGIA TERRITORY SO THAT 3,500 UN TROOPS FROM THE AFRICAN CONGO, INDIA AND OTHERS CAN PARACHUTE DOWN FROM THE SKIES UPON GEORGIA SOIL AND OCCUPY 1,500,000 ACRES OF THE SOVEREIGN STATE OF GEORGIA. (Some of these troops could be the BUTCHERS who murdered and raped the CHRISTIAN PRO-AMERICA KATANGANESE citizens.) These NATO exercises are to start, we understand, March 4 and last to March 22. The second NATO exercise in the same area will involve 17,000 FOREIGN TROOPS in June, 1963. . . .
>
> We believe that all of these co-called NATO MANEUVERS ARE PART OF THE IMPLEMENTATION OF THE TREASONOUS DISARMAMENT LAW, AND THESE FOREIGN TROOPS ENTERING THESE UNITED STATES IN THIS HUGE TROJAN HORSE RUSE WILL NEVER LEAVE OUR SHORES ONCE THEY ARE PERMITTED TO MAKE THESE ILLEGAL, UNLAWFUL LANDINGS UPON OUR SOIL AND "OCCUPY" OUR SOVEREIGN STATES. . . .

The United Nations and the North Atlantic Treaty Organization had nothing to do with Water Moccasin III. It was a United States Army training operation. The foreign student officers were representing only their own countries, all considered friendly to the U.S. The whole business about a Communist controlling UN "military forces" was pure malarkey.

On February 22, nonetheless, a group called The Conservatives, in Savannah, Georgia, reported the following in its weekly, *The Bulletin Board:*

> Georgia has had Soviet planes overhead. . . . Now she is to have guerrillas from fifteen nations simulating a take-over of part of our state. . . . Are we, like Pavlov's dogs, being conditioned for the real thing, a United Nations take-over?

Portions of The Conservatives' report were picked up and circulated in a flier (three cents each, 50 for $1.25) by The Network of Patriotic Letter Writers in Pasadena, California.

Near the end of February, a "Calling All Patriots" letter, written by retired Marine General Pedro A. del Valle, began appearing in the mail. The letter was later printed in *Task Force,* the publication of the Defenders of the American Constitution, Inc. It read, in part:

. . . the undersigned is convinced this [exercise] . . . signifies re-
hearsals of the UN take-over of the U.S.A. under the disarmament
treaty promulgated under public Law No. 87-297. . . . The urgency of
this message is obvious. *This appears to be the beginning of a crash
program to disarm the U.S.A. and make us a province of the UN.*
May God in His mercy help us to prevent this catastrophe!

On February 27, a United States Congressman, James B. Utt of
California, got into the act via his regular *Washington Report* newsletter:

NOW HEAR THIS AND LISTEN WELL! By the time this Washington Report reaches you, there will be under way one of the most
fantastic and, to me, truly frightening military maneuvers ever to
be held in the United States. It is called "Exercise Water Moccasin
III," and is just as deadly.

Congressman Utt went on to state that "Pentagon Intelligence"
had denied any knowledge of the operation, that a UN contingent would
be on hand and that "this operation comes squarely under Article 43 of
the United Nations Charter." (Article 43, dealing with a permanent
international peace force, has never been invoked.) To these unfounded
charges, Utt added the perfect fillip, the vivid bit of detail on which
rumors thrive:

We do not know whether African troops will be involved or not,
but we do know that there is a large contingent of barefooted Africans
that have been moved into Cuba for training in guerrilla warfare.
I would like to quote a few lines from 13-year-old Anna Maria Del-
gado, who escaped from Cuba:

"I went to a church school. They closed it about a year ago. The
Russians and all sorts of foreigners moved in. . . . Then about three
weeks ago, these Africans came. . . . They're always barefooted and
they wear short skirts that come just above their knees. They have
big rings in their ears and noses. . . . "

Who brought these Africans to Cuba? Was it the United Nations?
Was it Russia? Or was it the United States? . . .

Congressman Utt granted permission to anyone who received his
newsletter to quote all or any part of it. The Keep America Committee,
in Los Angeles, reprinted and circulated it (free of charge) throughout
California. The Network of Patriotic Letter Writers reprinted and
distributed it (two cents each, 100 for $1.75) throughout the nation.
Something called the Americans United Council, in Long Beach,
California, picked it up too. John Birch Society bookstores, such as the
American Opinion Library in Palo Alto and another in Santa Barbara,
California, passed these reprints around still further. The *Arizona
Newsletter*, in Phoenix, reprinted it, adding these words: "WHY has

our local newspaper refused to print this information? . . . WRITE your Senator and Representative for more information. ASK him these Questions.—WHY! WHY! WHY!"

Congressman Utt's newsletter also appeared in any number of right-wing publications, such as the *Santa Ana Register*, a daily newspaper in Orange County, California, with a circulation of 76,000; Kent Courtney's *Independent American* newspaper in New Orleans; the *Weekly Crusader*, published by Billy James Hargis and his Christian Crusade; the *Bible Institute News* in Oklahoma City; something called *Motivate* in Butler, Wisconsin, and something else called *On Target*, the official publication of the Minutemen. It appeared, too, in the *Congressional Record*.

Thousands and thousands of letters began to pour into Washington offices, asking "WHY! WHY! WHY!" In the midst of this barrage, the U.S. Army retreated. It cancelled plans for voluntary civilian participation, because of a "general misunderstanding" by the public concerning the intent of the mock guerrilla-warfare operation. How this affected some local Georgians was movingly described by Fred Eden, publisher of the *Claxton Enterprise*, on the *CBS Reports* telecast, *Case History of a Rumor*.

> The day came for the thing [Water Moccasin III] to begin . . . something had happened. And they came to tell us that they had been severely curtailed. . . . There wouldn't be the civilian participation that they had originally anticipated. . . . We asked them: Where did the problems arise? . . . And they said that there had been considerable criticism . . . written to our congressmen; and they had definitely cut back on the things that they would be allowed to do as part of this Operation. I guess maybe having spent over a year . . . overseas during World War II and flying several missions over Germany and then spending part of that time as a prisoner of war over there, I got some pretty corny ideas about patriotism. . . . This is what prompted me to feel that I had to say what I felt about this thing, and if somebody had stopped the training that I was to receive, maybe I would never have made it back. That's what it looked to me like was happening to these boys who were trying to train to fight . . . these brush-fire wars that we are having nowadays. And if those boys couldn't receive the practical training they needed right here, maybe they wouldn't make it back either.

But the affair was by no means ended. The rumormongers were only just getting warmed up. They displayed their virtuosity by ringing in anti-Semitism, race bias, atheism, fluoridation and the income tax. By mid-March many of the letter writers had naked cannibals marching through Georgia, with foreign troops prowling the nation. In a "special" newsletter, the Americans United Council, P.O. Box 2688, Long Beach, California, warned:

ALERT and ACTION   ALERT and ACTION
Red, White and Blue   URGENT—FAST   Red, White and Blue

To AMERICANS ONLY:
RE: *"OPERATION—WATER MOCCASIN III"*

> *Your Country, your Native Land—the UNITED STATES OF AMERICA—has just been invaded by military troops of foreign lands!* . . .
> Advices come from Maryland, Georgia, South Carolina, Texas, Washington, D.C.   Here are quotes: . . .
> "AFRICANS LANDING IN SAVANNAH (Georgia). Advance contingent of the UNITED NATIONS combat troops of Ghana and India from Katanga duty. . . . As many negro troops as others. . . . "
> While no schedule is yet available, an alert received states that FOREIGN MILITARY FORCES WILL MANEUVER THE WEST COASTAL STATES OF WASHINGTON, OREGON and CALIFORNIA. In view of the known CHINESE RED and MONGOLIAN TROOPS across the Mexican and Canadian borders, plus the probability of more offshore and in the hills on acreage purchased by Orientals—some of whom are naturalized and call themselves AMERICANS—the above may be of special significance now.

Even today, the reverberations have not ceased. Many months after the event, Republican Senator Thomas Kuchel of California, who denounced the "fright peddlers" shortly after the exercise, was still getting chiding letters from people who swallowed "Water Moccasin" whole.* Indeed, the hoax has taken an honored place in the folklore of extremism. Many Americans are still convinced that only their fervor prevented this nation's surrender to United Nations forces spearheaded by those cannibals with rings in their noses. A great many more still contend that *something* sinister, with or without naked cannibals, took place in Georgia.

---

*See the next reading selection, Chapter Four.

Chapter Four

The Reaction to the Far Right

After disclosures about the nature of the John Birch Society in 1961, the press of the nation began to document the activities of various extreme rightist groups. Articles fanned interest in the subject, and naturally enough, publications, government officials and citizens in general found it incumbent upon themselves to take a stand either for or against the rightist groups. For the most part there was little support for the activities of the extremists. Congressman John Rousselot, who admitted membership in the John Birch Society, naturally commended its activities, as did a few other members of the national government. But most of the reaction of officialdom and the general press was negative. To the rightist, this only proved the extent to which the press and the government were either in sympathy with communist aims or dupes of the world-wide conspiracy.

Probably nowhere was the reaction against the right more violent than in Congress. Under the blanket of Congressional immunity, a number of Representatives and Senators attacked the extreme right and especially the John Birch Society, often calling the rightists "Fascists" and likening Robert Welch to Adolph Hitler. Stung by the allegations concerning the Eisenhower administrations, Republicans were as vociferous in their denunciations as were Democrats, many of whom had become used to being labeled "subversive" during the McCarthy Era. The first group of articles in this chapter chronicles this reaction in the Senate.

It goes without saying that the American liberal press has from the first had little use for the antics of the extreme right. Magazines like the *Nation, New Republic* and the *Reporter,* religious periodicals like *Christian Century* and *Commonweal,* and major liberal metropolitan dailies have been denouncing what they often call the "lunatic fringe" for years. More interesting only because less expected have been the denunciations of the extreme right by solidly conservative publications. Here the common point of view has been that the extremists are undermining the cause of true conservatism, and are also hindering America's contest with the Soviet Union by sowing distrust for all of our institutions. The conservative press response to the far right is indicated by two selections. Several statements by J. Edgar Hoover complete the chapter.

The Fright Peddlers*

Senator Thomas Kuchel

One of the longest and most impressive assaults on the right was a speech titled "The Fright Peddlers," delivered in the Senate by Republican Thomas Kuchel of California on May 2, 1963. Kuchel's speech was especially valuable because of the many quotes from rightists that he used. One can get some insight into the mind of the rank-and-file rightist from the letters written to Kuchel about Exercise Water Moccasin.

The American people are keenly aware of the grave and evil hazards to our freedom and to our way of life which international communism is eternally dedicated to destroy.

Aside from a relative handful of traitorous zealots in the ranks or clutches of the Communist Party, we—all of us in this land—are unalterably committed to deter and, if necessary, to combat and defeat any aggression, Communist or otherwise, against us or our free friends, who, like us, propose to keep our freedom.

I rise today to speak of another danger we confront, not as dread or as foreboding, but equally offensive and evil to all reasonable, rational, free American citizens.

It is the danger of hate and venom, of slander and abuse, generated by fear and heaped indiscriminately upon many great Americans by another relative handful of zealots, in the ranks or clutches of self-styled "I am a better American than you are" organizations.

It results from a strange intellectual strabismus which professes to see our government crawling with Communists and which, abandoning the processes of reason, pours its spleen upon anything or anybody which does not meet its own queer and puzzling dogmas.

Mr. President, in every day's deluge of mail at my office, which sometimes means as many as 5,000 letters, telegrams, and postcards

---

*Congressional Record, 88th Congress, Sess. I, pp. 7636–41.

—there are generally a hundred and even two hundred letters which I describe simply as "fright mail."

Most of my colleagues receive such mail and most of them refer to it in much stronger terms. Coming from the most populous state in our Union, California, I think it is safe to say I get as much as anybody.

It is difficult enough attempting to answer thousands and thousands of letters which seek fifteen answers to fifteen questions on complicated foreign and domestic policies and issues—and by tomorrow at the latest.

Many times, the only economically and mechanically feasible way to reply is to send printed statements, which are then often returned in disgust because I have not answered with a long, personal letter.

But, Mr. President, that is a minor problem compared to what to do about the "fright mail."

I know this is a matter which many of my colleagues have given a lot of thought to privately, but, so far as I know, no one has discussed publicly.

I cheerfully admit that I have, in the past, attempted to reply calmly and factually to "fright mail," mustering all the reason and reserve I could summon.

Yet, I have found over the years that this is not quite the answer.

For most fright mail writers will come right back a week later, terrified about something else, urgently stating that they do not believe me—and that I am either misinformed or worse. Sometimes, they darkly insinuate that treason has prompted the reply they have received.

Treason. I still cannot believe my eyes when I stare at the ugliest word in the American lexicon tossed about in a letter as casually as the "Dear Senator" salutation which opens it. Indeed, I was once charged with treason by a correspondent who then closed his letter a few words later with "Respectfully yours."

Treason. The most heinous crime on the American books. And not always scrawled illiterately on a scrap of a paper bag, but often typed meticulously on embossed paper.

In recent months, I have been casually accused of ignorance or of a desire to sell my country down the river because I have said for example, that it not only seemed untrue on its face, but was demonstrably untrue, that thousands and thousands of Chinese Communist troops were poised on the Mexican border for an attack on California.

It not only seemed untrue on its face, but was demonstrably untrue that such-and-such American or free world leader—forty-four of them in all—is a Communist agent. The gallant Eisenhower is a favorite target for their contemptible slime.

What new and frightening charge tomorrow's mail will bring, I cannot begin to anticipate.

But I do want to disclose the two latest and intertwined "frights" —and analyze them in detail—by quoting in its entirety a typical letter I received in recent days.

The letter, on good stationery and carefully typed, comes from a constituent who lives high in the Berkeley hills in California. It is somewhat mild in its intimations of treason, but otherwise is sadly typical. It reads as follows:

DEAR SENATOR KUCHEL:

Thanks for your reply of March 9 regarding the Disarmament Agency.

I do not accept your statement that I have been the victim of misinformation. It is the other way around. Either you do not know what you have voted for in Public Law 87-297, or you are a traitor to the United States.

I would suggest you get in touch with Mr. Theodore Jackman, box 10188, Greenville, S.C. He is an expert on this subject. I had the pleasure of hearing him here in Berkeley a few days ago. Undoubtedly, he will be more than glad to come and talk with you about United Nations control over the United States of America, disarmament, and so forth.

Right at the present time, the U.S. Army is conducting operations in Georgia—Operation Moccasin—which many citizens over the country believe is a prelude and a training exercise for the take-over of the United States in the very near future, under United Nations authority. Of course, due to the large protest from citizens, the Army is denying everything.

Senator Kuchel, you better study up on what's going on. You have gone on record to me that I am under a misapprehension that we are being unilaterally disarmed. If this country is taken over by the United Nations, I will personally label you a traitor.

You better study up on what's going on in this country.

Sincerely yours,

Mr. President, note carefully the language, typical of the fright letter. The writer is convinced, utterly convinced. There is no room for doubt. Of course, this is happening, he says; and, of course, that is happening, he says. Because "he knows." And how did he find out? And how, if it is possible, can we reach him with simple truth?

First, let us look at what is the simple truth.

Here is an editorial from the *Claxton* (Ga.) *Enterprise*, a weekly newspaper published in the area where Operation Water Moccasin was held. It is entitled "Fear of Snakes."
It reads as follows:

A national furor has been raised over the Army exercise recently underway here, known as Water Moccasin III. Our office has received numerous letters from such places as Richmond, Savannah, New Orleans, and Minneapolis—all expressing a grave dread over the operation.

Evidently a lot of folks are scared of snakes, and in their sick minds anything with the name of a snake conjures up visions of a viper or a man-eating reptile that sets them off on weird fantasies that defy description.

One Congressman went so far as to suggest that the United States was training "barefooted Africans as guerrilla warriors," to be used to subjugate other African nations.

Another had it figured that the United Nations was sending in foreign troops to be trained to overthrow our Government. Another decided we were being trained in how to surrender our cities to insurgents.

Still another imagined all of this area being "invaded by hordes of Mongolians" who were overrunning the entire area.

It is fantastic what the human mind can dream up over the simple statement that a few foreign students will act as observers in the operation. We were in almost daily contact with an English major and an Italian police officer. We also were visited by an Army team that had a Turkish officer as an observer. But we missed out on the "hordes of foreign Communists."

Some of the statements we have read amount to hysteria, the result of a sick mind, carried away by the self-induced hallucinations. Our experience with the people involved directly in the operation left us with the feeling that we were taking part in some important training that may one day aid our Nation in its struggle for world peace against a foe that uses all sorts of unorthodox tactics. We are glad to know that we have people in our Armed Forces with the ability and training that these men showed during our observation of this operation.

We look forward to Operation No. IV, but we suggest that the Army change the name to Primrose Path IV—or Azalea Trail or some such title—Water Moccasin IV seems to make people dream bad dreams, and act like dope addicts.

The editorial demonstrates, rather savagely, but correctly, I think, the irrational frenzy of my correspondent's claims about Operation

Water Moccasin, alleged Army subversion and United Nations take-over of the United States.

I shall send my frightened constituent a copy of it. But will it really convince him? Perhaps, perhaps not. The *Claxton Enterprise* could be some clever sort of Communist front, my constituent may suspect.

But what is really frightening, is that I shall also have to send a copy of the editorial to several thousand similarly frightened Californians who have fallen hook, line and sinker for the Operation Water Moccasin "plot" and have asked me to do all I can to halt the operation, if I am a decent American, with any courage at all.

Just listen to some sample quotes from my mail on Operation Water Moccasin:

From Hermosa Beach:

> Last night, in Los Angeles, I heard a talk by Mr. Theodore Jack-man of Greenville, S.C., about a frightening military maneuver now being held in the state of Georgia, called Exercise Water Moccasin III. It is time Congress demands the facts about Exercise Water Moccasin III, the United Nations War Operations and NATO Operations.

From San Jose:

> I am writing you this letter of protest, to the presence of foreign troops on American soil. That there are African Negro troops, who are cannables [sic], stationed in Georgia.

From Hollywood:

> It is unconstitutional to quarter American troops in American homes, so how come these pagan, ruthless, brutal, Godless savages? Yes, we know of the UN plans to place Mongolian and Congolese troops over our dear United States (the same kind of troops which ravished Katanga) if the UN can swing their damnable world police force plan, so undoubtedly these Moccasin troops are to be the same.

From Paradise:

> From friends in the state of Georgia, I have a report that at this time there are 15,000 United Nations personnel from 15 countries, participating in what is known as Operation Water Moccasin.

From Westminster, near my home town:

> I also understand there are oriental troops in Mexico at this moment waiting to "occupy" parts of California for their training.

From Berkeley:

> The news has just broken, although there had been rumors for a week or more, that Georgia is the place for 16,000 African soldiers,

being trained by the UN for guerrilla warfare. Complete with nose and ear rings. This time, the UN, and our State Department, have gone too far.

From Sacramento, the capital of my state:

This morning on radio, over Mr. Beirpos' program, I heard the most fantastic thing I have ever heard. Water Moccasin—what is this secret fantastic thing going on in the Deep South. UN troops coming to America for some kind of a "war to invade America." Mr. Senator, these things are being said over the radio, and he would not say them if they were not true. He said, "it's a three-point program of the disarmament program."

From Los Angeles:

Water Moccasin—we are asking you to give us a report on what you are doing to protect our constitutional rights. Also repeal income taxes.

From Los Angeles:

I am greatly disturbed at the news of foreign troops on our soil, as in Water Moccasin III. I am convinced we must get out of the United Nations. There is no longer any doubt that it is dominated by the Communists.

From Los Angeles:

I have just heard about one of the most fantastic and truly frightening military maneuvers ever to be held in the United States. The Oxford, Miss., invasion and violence was illegal and completely unconstitutional. I feel the United Nations is responsible. The UN is no good. Let's get out of it—now. I'm still sick from the Katanga tragedy.

From Ontario:

These so-called war games are in reality a deceitful way of bringing in the troops that will be used to enforce United Nations law on U.S. citizens. What are you doing about this? Let's get out of the godless United Nations and kick it out of the United States of America.

Mr. President, just think of it—"cannibals stationed in Georgia," they have charged:

Pagan, ruthless, brutal godless savages, Mongolian and Congolese troops—world police plan. Fifteen thousand United Nations troops already here. Oriental troops in Mexico, waiting to occupy California. Sixteen thousand African troops, already in Georgia, with rings in their noses and ears. A war to invade America. A United Nations takeover. Integration, part of the disarmament program. Let's get out of the UN. Investigate NATO.

And abolish income taxes, too—if, presumably, there is still time. *(Laughter.)*

Frightening is not the word for it. It is incredible.

It is incredible that so many Americans have been so cruelly swindled, and have allowed themselves to be so deceitfully duped, about a U.S. Army troop exercise instructing our soldiers in counter-guerrilla warfare—and witnessed, incidentally, by 124, not 15,000 or 16,000, foreign military officers from Canada, the Republic of China, France, Great Britain, Guatemala, Indonesia, Iran, Italy, Japan, South Korea, Liberia, Pakistan, the Philippines, Spain, Thailand, Turkey, and Vietnam.

Now who and what whips up so many Americans to a state of frenzy and despair over such "conspiracies" as the U.S. Army's "sellout to the United Nations" under the "direction of the Arms Control Agency."

The answers are not hard to find.

Two of my cited correspondents indicated a mysterious "Mr. Jackman, of Greenville, South Carolina," has contributed.

Others—as do many of my frightened correspondents—enclosed for my edification another definite source—an ignorant, crude, and equally hysterical leaflet.

I ask unanimous consent that the leaflet be printed at this point in the *Record*.

There being no objection, the leaflet was ordered to be printed in the *Record*, as follows:

The United States Has No Army, No Navy, No Air Force

For doubting Thomases who think this statement is not true, Senate bill No. 2180[1] entitled "The Arms Control and Disarmament Act" was approved by the House of Representatives as House bill 9118[2] and was signed into effect as Public Law 87-297 on September 26, 1961[3], by John F. Kennedy, President of the United States. This bill was prepared to expedite a plan already proposed at Geneva by our administration and State Department (see Publication No. 7277 for full particulars of its terms) to effect the "legal" connotation to disarmament.

The only thing that keeps our Army, Navy, and Air Force from being wiped out of existence is public opinion. At any time he chooses the President of the United States can now transfer our Army, Navy,

---

[1] See *Congressional Record*, p. 17590, Sept. 8, 1961.

[2] See *Congressional Record*, pp. 19038–19104, Sept. 19, 1961 (first vote)—p. 19640, Sept. 23, 1961 (final and approval).

[3] See *Congressional Record*, p. 10912, Sept. 28, 1961.

and Air Force (your husband, father, son, or brother) to the command of Eugeny D. Kiselev (Russian) who is Secretary of the United Nations Security Council (World Police Force).

. . . .

Attributed to secret agreement between Alger Hiss and Molotov confirmed by Trygve Lie[4] and U.S. State Department[5] and verified by subsequent action, the Secretary of the United Nations Security Council (who is in command of the United Nations Military Secretariat (World Police Force)[6] must always be a Russian.

Here is the record: 1946–49, Arkady S. Sobelov,[7] U.S.S.R.; 1950–53, Konstantine Zinchenko,[8] U.S.S.R.; 1953–57, Ilya Tchernyshev, U.S.S.R.; 1957–60, A. Dobrynin, U.S.S.R.; 1960–62, George P. Arkadev,[9] U.S.S.R.; 1962– --, Eugeny D. Kiselev, U.S.S.R.

Prepared by: United Societies of Methodist Laymen, Inc., Austin, Texas.

That is the leaflet. It is very much like the dozens of allegedly "patriotic" fliers and pamphlets and leaflets which pour into my office by the hundreds, attached to frantic, pleading, threatening messages, sometimes typed on the finest stationery.

It is distressing and disillusioning to find persons of normal educational attainments—or any educational level—falling hysterically and emotionally, without reservations, for the unadulterated venom spewed by out-and-out crackpots for paranoia and profit.

It is disgusting to find self-appointed saviors, whether infantile and psychotically on the fears of Americans in the name of anti-communism. Indeed, the ugly labors they perform are a service to the Kremlin itself. They seek to divide and too often succeed in dividing, our people, far better than any Communist agents could do.

---

[4] Pp. 45–46 of his book *In the Cause of Peace* (New York: Macmillan, 1954).

[5] Bulletin No. 422A, dated August 2, 1947.

[6] Articles 46, 47 of United Nations Charter.

[7] Had Lt. Gen. A. Ph. Vasiliev as chairman of the Military Staff Committee—the same man who was in charge of a report containing recommendations of the general principles governing the organization of the Armed Forces made available to the Security Council by member nations of the United Nations, and the same man who was granted a leave of absence after setting up this organization to serve as adviser to North Korean Communists during the Korean War, in charge of all movements across the 38th parallel and from the evidence indicates that he knew what the U.S. troops would do before MacArthur was given his orders by Zinchenko.

[8] Screened military directives to Gen. Douglas MacArthur during the Korean police action.

[9] Screened and ordered Congo-Katanga directives and had more to say than you did that American planes be used to destroy anti-Communists in the Congo.

Day in and day out, every Senator and every Government official I know works long, hard hours devoted to one primary mission:

To protect and promote the security, welfare, and best interests of one country and one country alone—the United States of America, a country all of us in this Chamber unashamedly revere.

Do these people really believe, I ask myself—and now I ask them—that a gigantic and incredible and unprecedented conspiracy has occurred in America in which the President and his Cabinet, 99 per cent of the Congress, 99 per cent of the nation's journalists, and even the U.S. Army have all taken part to sell out our country?

Do they really believe further that this conspiracy is visible only to a small number of self-appointed saviors, such as Mr. Jackman?

If they do, the only reasonable reply I can give to them which they will understand is the honorable, 100 per cent red, white, and blue expression: "Nuts."

Who, we might also ask, is this Mr. Jackman? He is simply the Reverend Theodore Jackman, an available speaker for the American Opinion Speakers Bureau, the "nationwide conservative speakers' exchange" run by the John Birch Society, whose major contribution to the security and welfare of the United States of America was to "unmask" Dwight Eisenhower as a traitor.

Speaking of that highly publicized organization, I digress for a moment to point out to my colleagues, who may not have heard, that the founder of the Birch group has recently revised the party line viewpoint on former President Eisenhower—at least somewhat.

According to newspaper reports, the latest reprints of the founder's memorable book, *The Politician*, now gives followers the following choice—

> That he—Eisenhower—is a mere stooge, or that he is a Communist assigned the specific job of being a political front man.

But the ludicrous word from high up in the Birch councils on the late former Secretary of State John Foster Dulles, of course, remains: "I personally believe Dulles to be a Communist agent," the founder of the Birch Society continues to profess.

As Ripley said, "believe it or not."

But, returning to the leaflet, I have received so far more than 2,000 letters demanding abolition of the U.S. Arms Control Agency on the grounds cited in the leaflet. Indeed, several hundred constituents have sent to me this leaflet, or variations of it.

And the most depressing statistics of all are as follows:

Only four constituents have raised even the slightest doubt at all about the leaflet's validity—as only six even considered at all the possibility the Operation Water Moccasin fright was a hoax.

To the first few hundred constituents who wrote to me in panic that the Arms Control Act transfers our military to a Russian colonel, I observed mildly, they were victims of misinformation.

As my colleagues know, the forerunner of the U.S. Arms Control and Disarmament Agency was the Disarmament Administration, which was established under former President Eisenhower.

As my colleagues also know, strong support for the legislation to establish the Arms Control Agency was offered in testimony by such distinguished American leaders as Gen. Alfred M. Gruenther, former supreme commander of NATO; Gen. Lyman L. Lemnitzer, former Chairman of the Joint Chiefs of Staff and now supreme commander of NATO; Henry Cabot Lodge, my party's candidate for Vice President and a good American; Christian Herter, an able, dedicated American and Republican who serves the present administration as he did the last; and Robert Lovett, capable former Secretary of Defense.

Quoting from the report of the Committee on Foreign Relations of the U.S. Senate:

> The (Arms Control) Agency is to be responsible, under the direction of the Secretary of State, for the acquisition of a fund of practical and theoretical knowledge about disarmament and is directed to conduct research in that field, to engage public or private institutions or persons for such studies, and to coordinate work in this field now being undertaken by other Government agencies in accordance with procedures to be established by the President.

And so, the Foreign Relations Committee of the U.S. Senate, composed of eleven Democrats and six Republicans, unanimously went on record in favor of the legislation.

I told my frightened constituents all of this.

I told them that the Arms Control Agency, endorsed by an overwhelming Senate vote of 73 to 14 in 1961, has no power to disarm our country; that the only authority it has is to conduct research on matters of arms control and the effect of any reduction in the level of armaments on various parts of our economy; that it reports to the President and does not act independently; that its function is merely to bring the best talent available so that our representatives and the President can deal effectively with arms control matters; and that no responsible public official believes in unilateral disarmament or disarmament without an effective means of inspection.

What was the result? More leaflets in return, even wilder than the first batch. Plus, new or renewed accusations as to what is prompting my answers.

Let me cite some of the further authority or proof they sent on: I ask unanimous consent that the text of that creed be printed in the *Record* in full.

There being no objection, the leaflet was ordered to be printed in the *Record*, as follows:

The Handwriting on the Wall: Soon You Will Not Be a Citizen of a Free America

The U.S. Congress has passed a law, No. 87–297, which established an office of dictator. This office to be filled by appointment, appointment by the President.

The appointee is not called dictator: he is called Director of Disarmament and Arms Control.

He shall give his orders to the Secretary of State and to the President; and they shall see that his orders are carried out.

There shall be no jurisdiction over him: neither by the President, nor by the Congress.

The Director shall collaborate with, and receive orders from Eugene Kiselev (Russian), the Secretary of the United Nations.

All the U.S. arsenals and conveyances; missiles, planes, tanks, and ships are through his orders to be placed at the disposal of the UN Secretary. Then, all military centers are to be dismantled, and all American military personnel discharged. But afterward, discharged Americans will be drafted by the United Nations, to serve it, in far-away places.

For your free America will be only a vassal state under the UN. Uncle Sam cannot then move his finger, without permission from the United Nations. But Khrushchev and Russia always veto everything Uncle Sam requests. So then the UN will never favor the United States of America under any condition whatever.

Law 87–297 is operating. William C. Foster is the Director. Five atomic submarines, Polaris submarines have been given to the UN. They have been definitely promised the UN by the President and Secretary McNamara, and airbases are frequently being dismantled. Law 87–297 makes Foster subject to no law, nor to any authoritative body.

You will not have your job, nor your home, neither your self. If your Congress is not awakened and caused to repeal Public Law 87–297 soon. It must be repealed very soon.

Let it be understood also, that there are deputy directors, and many more will be appointed. There will be these appointed officials over the entire country; and there will be no civil courts; neither any civil officers to appeal to: for these deputies' orders will supersede orders of all civil officers.

Sounds fantastic. Then listen: The UN did not help the liberty-loving people of Hungary. The UN stood by and watched the savage Communist hordes massacre the people of Hungary. The UN has harassed and caused atrocities to be committed upon the best and only great people of the Congo. The UN has never helped any liberty-loving people. The UN despises God. What is fantastic truly is that you are a personality: yet you do not know when you began to be: yet you have a destiny—and do not know where you are headed.

While you and I were overwhelmed with the many machinations of the modern era: the oneworlders, through their never-tiring kibitzers overwhelmed most of your Congress, and pressured them into surrendering your Government.

And who is William C. Foster, Director of Disarmament who has this great power? He is not only a member of the ruling power, the Council on Foreign Relations, but a Director of this Council. And who is Col. Marshall Sanders, U.S. Air Force—on active duty in the Air Force? He is the colonel assigned by the Air Force to serve this Council on Foreign Relations for one year. He is listed in the annual report of the Council on Foreign Relations for 1962–63 as Air Force research fellow. This should convince anyone who rules the country today.

(Send to the U.S. Flag Committee, Post Office Box 269, Jackson Heights, N.Y., for report on this Council on Foreign Relations, $1.)

Observe, there is that Russian colonel again, ever ubiquitous in "running the UN's military operations" and getting ready to take over our Armed Forces, plus our jobs, our homes and our very selves.

It is simply impossible to take the time and energy to prove demonstrably the outright falsehood of every zany claim alleged by this leaflet—from the giving of atomic submarines to the UN to William Foster's supposedly being subject to no law.

But consider the key and most frightening plank in these leaflets—the charge that a Russian colonel is commanding or will command all of our military. Can its origin be found?

Yes, it can. It can be found word for word in, of all things, a stage play written in the early 1950's by one Myron C. Fagan, the national director of something in Hollywood called the Cinema Educational Guild. The play, titled *Thieves' Paradise*, purported to show, in Fagan's own words:

Why we must get the United States out of the UN—and the UN out of the United States . . . [revealing] all the different phases of the diabolical plot—how the UN was a "Trojan Horse" sneaked into the United States to serve as a sanctuary for Red spies, saboteurs and American traitors . . . how it was to destroy our freedoms through "treaties" such as "genocide" and the "World Court" . . . to brainwash our youth through UNESCO and UNICEF, etc. . . . to drain us of our wealth through UNRAA, the Marshall plan, and our foreign aid give-aways . . . and finally to transform the United States into an enslaved unit of their Communist one-world government.

In a little green tract, titled "UN Tract No. 1," from which I just read, Fagan and the Cinema Educational Guild quotes the following dialog from his play:

> Stefan. When they were setting up the UN, Molotov and Alger Hiss made a secret agreement that the military chief of the UN was always to be a Russian, appointed by Moscow. The first such Chief was Arkady Sobelov.
>
> Rita. I know—
>
> Stefan. But do you know why Moscow wanted that arrangement? (Rita shakes her head—Stefan explains gloatingly) To be prepared, if the UN would have to interfere in any Communist attempts to grab free states their man would have charge of that interference and—
>
> Rita. (Breaks in—suddenly understands) and their man would be able to keep the Red commanders fully informed of all the plans and movements of the UN forces?

There it is. The basis for the charge that a Russian colonel is going to command our military.

Now, first, who is Myron Fagan, who discovered this vile plot so many years ago?

I quote briefly from portions of the eleventh report of the State Senate Fact-finding Subcommittee on Un-American Activities to the 1961 regular California Legislature:

> We do not wish to impugn the sincerity of Mr. Fagan, but we do wish to make public the facts about his Cinema Educational Guild, and our opinion concerning the erroneous nature of many of the statements contained in its publications. . . . There are heavy evidences of anti-Semitism throughout many of the booklets and in many of the Fagan speeches. . . . Mr. Fagan may well be one of the Nation's outstanding experts on matters theatrical, but that does not necessarily qualify him as an expert in the field of countersubversive intelligence.

So there we have it. The daisy chain is complete.

And what the fright peddlers have handed down to one another, over the years, is a daisy of a whopper, a puerile and evil package of fright calculated to "scare the daylights" out of decent Americans. This whopper has been debunked thoroughly over the years. Yet, here it is again. And not only in letters and leaflets. Let me quote from an item in the April, 1963, issue of the despicable *The Cross and The Flag*, the anti-Semitic hate sheet of Gerald L. K. Smith:

UN Military Dictatorship

The world police force of the United Nations is run by a Communist carrying the title "Secretary of the UN Security Council." Since the beginning of the United Nations a Russian Communist has held this authoritative position of top UN military authority.

Below are the names of Soviet agents who have held this position to the exclusion of all other nations:

1946 to 1949: Arkady S. Sobelov, U.S.S.R.

1950 to 1953: Konstantine Zinchenko, U.S.S.R. Screened military directives to Gen. Douglas MacArthur during Korean police action.

1953 to 1957: Ilya Tchernyshev, U.S.S.R.

1957 to 1960: A. Dobrynin, U.S.S.R.

1960 to 1962: George P. Arkadev, U.S.S.R. Screened Congo-Katanga directives Eugeny D. Kiselev, U.S.S.R.

Or let me quote just a few paragraphs from a news item in the *Long Beach* (Calif.) *Independent*, a metropolitan daily newspaper, of March 15, 1963:

The U.S. Government is trying to put all its armed forces under the command of a Russian general, John Rousselot told 600 persons in municipal auditorium Thursday night.

Rousselot, John Birch Society district governor for six western states and former Congressman from California's 25th District, spoke on "Disarmament—Blueprint for Surrender."

This office [referring to Under-Secretary for Security Council and Political Affairs] is held by a Russian general, he said, and if the United States turns its armed forces to the UN, the Russian general will command them.

Those fantastic charges, Mr. President, are false—completely false.

But when one, who was honored to be a Member of the Congress of the United States for two years—or even one who writes for an undisguised hate sheet, utters such a cry, there are Americans who listen and believe.

The facts are that our American Military Establishment is American and shall remain so. We joined the United Nations because we believe in and work for peace with justice in the world. Where the

United Nations has sought to quell aggression, the United States has played its honorable role.

There is no Russian colonel, or general, or military or civilian individual who is "secretary of the United Nations" or "secretary of the UN Security Council."

Let the record be clear that there are nineteen undersecretaries of the Security Council, of which thirteen are filled by Americans or representatives of our allies and of which two are Soviet bloc nations.

None of them has anything to do with the command of any joint UN military operations. There is no world police force in the UN. And, of course, no Soviet national ever gave General Douglas MacArthur any orders.

How hysterical and idiotic can one get? I am afraid to answer, until I have seen tomorrow's mail.

Leaflets, of course, are not the only cause for hysteria.

Lunatic columnists, apostles of hate and fear on radio and television, and even loony letters to the editor provoke their share of fright mail.

The curious fact is that the fright peddlers, from the simple simpletons to the wretched racists, all claim to be conservatives.

They defile the honorable philosophy of conservatism with that claim as thoroughly as the Communists defile the honorable philosophy of liberalism.

I sympathize with some of my constituents who are honestly bewildered and confused by the trash of the right-wing extremists.

I even feel sympathetic with those who have been taken in as dupes.

But I have nothing but seething contempt for the originators of the hoaxes and swindles, from the ludicrous leaders of the Birch Society to the equally ludicrous director of the Cinema Educational Guild, including any and all of the several hundred similar self-styled patriotic groups.

They are anything but patriotic. Indeed, a good case can be made that they are unpatriotic, and downright un-American. For they are doing a devil's work far better than Communists themselves could do.

It is curious to me that they all have generally the same aims, issued in all-out, uncompromising, almost hysterical demands: Get the United States out of the UN. Stop all foreign aid. Repeal the income tax. Abandon NATO and bring our troops home from Europe.

It is ironic that these very aims are very likely identical to the real hopes and aspirations of the Kremlin.

At any rate, I could not imagine a program that would delight Khrushchev more.

•

For we have a United Nations, with imperfections to be sure, but a UN in which the Soviet Union has had to resort to a veto on 100 occasions, while we have never had to resort to a veto at all. We have a United Nations which the Soviet Premier has bitterly attacked on numerous occasions as U.S. controlled. A United Nations the Communists have never been able to control or subvert to their own use.

Yet, say the extremists, abandon it to the Communists.

Stop all foreign aid, the self-styled patriots say. Not some, not most, but all: military and economic. Let us stop helping to maintain two million free world troops on the perimeter of the Soviet Union, the patriots are really demanding. Let us write off every nation of the world as unrestricted fair game for the Communists, they are really saying. And if these countries need help in establishing military, and political and economic stability, let the Communists, or somebody else, provide it, they are really saying.

Repeal the income tax, they say. Not cut taxes, repeal them. And repeal our national defense, in the process.

Abandon NATO, they say. For the Birch leader has said:

> With regard to that brainchild of Dean Acheson, godchild of Harry Truman, and eventual ward of Dwight Eisenhower, we have repeatedly insisted for years that it was probably the biggest—and certainly one of the most expensive—hoax in all human history.

Abandon NATO, they say—and leave Europe to the whim or mercy of the Soviet Union.

It is an amazing paradox that the right-wing extremists find the same programs and organizations to be subversive that the left-wing extremists find to be the "tools and weapons of the Wall Street imperialists," as witness Communist Party literature on our mutual security programs and NATO.

Of late I have been receiving letters from Birchers and their fellow travelers calling for removal of American troops in Vietnam. And I have also been receiving letters from Communists, left-wingers, and their fellow travelers calling for precisely the same thing.

No, much as the fright peddlers, the right-wing extremists, and the Communists may desire such mutual goals, America is not going to bow to their dictates.

Let us, by all means, debate, as reasonable and rational and realistic people, the successes and failures of the United Nations and foreign aid.

But let us not do it on the basis of childish slogans or on the inane premise that they are Communist programs adopted by a Communist or pro-Communist government in Washington.

Our policies—American policies—are open to question and debate —as they must always be.

I am a Republican—and I shall continue to question the cold-war policies of a Democratic administration and fight those I consider unwise.

But both political parties—Republicans and Democrats—have the best interests of the country we love in mind and heart.

I wonder, however, about the fright peddlers and the followers of an organization whose founder has declared: "Democracy is merely a deceptive phrase, a weapon of demagoguery and a perennial fraud."

Clutching at half-truths and downright falsehoods, the fright peddlers fabricate hoaxes, as we have seen, which frighten Americans and divert their attention from the real menace. They sow suspicion and hatred. They attempt to undermine faith in government, its institutions, and its leaders. They preach resistance to the laws of our land. They degrade America and Americans, and do it as well as—or better than—the Communists do.

Yet, their followers—and even some honest conservatives—continually ask me: Why do I keep berating them, instead of the Communists?

I loathe and despise communism and Communists. By voice and by vote, all of my adult life I have attacked them and opposed them.

I expect the hoaxes and the spreading of hysteria, the sowing of suspicion, and the denigration of our government, institutions, and leaders from the camp of the enemy, communism, but not from fellow Americans.

I shall always fight the big lie, the smear, witch hunts, anti-Catholicism, anti-Semitism, racism of any kind—which are not the hallmarks of conservatism, but are the trademarks of communism and fascism.

I am concerned about right-wing extremists, not because of the noise they make, which, as with the vile Communists, is out of proportion to their size. I am concerned because they are, after all, Americans, not agents sworn to allegiance to a foreign power.

Astonishingly to me, I sometimes get letters from avowed Birchers who furiously deny their leader has ever charged the Central Intelligence Agency is Communist-controlled, or that Dulles was a Communist, or that NATO is a Communist-planned hoax.

And I find it equally hard to believe that the followers of the fright peddlers are all wholly oblivious to the anti-Semitism, anti-Catholicism, and outright racism of many of their "saviors."

I am going to read a letter of the kind which arrives now and again. I cite the letter not to "prove" that all right-wing extremists are bigots or that a majority are; I really do not know how many are, perhaps very few.

I cite it merely to show that this type of person, the follower of Myron Fagan and Gerald L. K. Smith, has often found a new, "respectable" home in an extremist right-wing group that denies being bigoted.

The letter, from Westminster, California, reads in part:

SIRS:

I am writing you again just to state that you can ignore me but you are sure not being ignored, your latest blast at Americans in the John Birch Society is just more evidence of your support of communism. I am a member of the Birch Society and I know many other members and every one of them are decent Americans who are interested in constitutional government and free enterprise and a real education for their children, and who mean to have it in spite of the grip that Jew communism that you support has on our country and Government. . . .

On this law by superior force that is called integration what do you think is going to be gained by that, the Jew press, radio, TV, and papers all scream the law of the land, who do you think believes it. . . . If you want integration let's start with the Jew schools. And synagogues. . . .

When are you going to stand up like a white man.

That is more than enough to illustrate my point—and to complete this autopsy.

My conclusion is simply this: Perhaps 10 per cent of the 60,000 letters I receive each month fall into the category of fright mail.

This mail flies in the face of a clear, stern, and pertinent warning from a great and dedicated American, J. Edgar Hoover, in February, 1962. Mr. Hoover then wrote in the *Journal of the American Bar Association:*

Today, far too many self-styled experts on communism are plying the highways of America, giving erroneous and distorted information. This causes hysteria, false alarms, misplaced apprehension by many of our citizens. We need enlightenment about communism but this information must be factual, accurate and not tailored to echo personal idiosyncrasies. To quote an old aphorism: We need more light and less heat.

Can these cruelly swindled victims of the fright peddlers be shocked into a reappraisal of their swindlers and be reclaimed as valuable and effective contributors in the fight against the real enemy? I do not know. But I believe it is time such an attempt be made. Perhaps I am naive about this. Yet I feel there must be some— and they belong to both political parties—who can be persuaded to join the ranks again of sensible and decent anti-Communist, pro-Americans devoted to defending our Nation against defilement of both the extreme left and extreme right, here and abroad.

America has enough immediate and deadly dangerous enemies, without manufacturing hobgoblins. America can use all the responsible help it can receive.

Danger from the Far Right*

Senator Stephen Young

Of all the members of Congress, none has addressed himself to the problem of the extreme right more often than Democratic Senator Stephen Young of Ohio, and nobody has used stronger language of denunciation. More than once he has posed the proposition which underlies the following speech, that the far right "is an even deadlier threat to our democratic traditions and institutions than are American adherents to communism." That is, of course, one of the central questions underlying the whole problem of the right—is it really a threat to the American government and way of life? The speech quoted here was given in the Senate on August 15, 1963.

In the past I have said that in my judgment the fascist John Birch Society and others like it are as serious a threat to our security and way of life as internal communism. Today I shall go even further. I believe that the radical right today is an even deadlier threat to our democratic traditions and institutions than are American adherents to communism.

American Communists try to infiltrate our political parties, our schools, our mass media, our labor unions—all institutions of the free society—in order to further the cause of the international Communist conspiracy. Their ability to achieve their purpose has diminished steadily over the past fifteen years through harassment by government

---

Congressional Record, 88th Congress, Sess. I, pp. 15178–80.

agencies and congressional committees and by exposure in the public press. It is estimated that today there are fewer than 10,000 Communist Party members in the nation. Of this total number—8,000 to 10,000 estimated by Director J. Edgar Hoover—I assert a considerable number are in reality counteragents—loyal Americans—who report regularly to our nation's FBI or CIA.

Although the danger from internal communism has been lessening, the radicals of the right—in Europe they would be called fascists —now pose a dangerous threat in trying to destroy the civil liberties and institutions which are the foundations of freedom. They accuse everyone who disagrees with their brand of "Americanism" of being a Communist or Communist sympathizer. They question the integrity of our Supreme Court. They stir resentment against our participation in the United Nations. They want the income tax repealed.

They try to block all foreign aid programs. They vilify foreign-born and minority-group American citizens. They spread seeds of suspicion in communities throughout the nation.

The great danger today rises from the fact that millions of well-meaning Americans embrace their programs as valid solutions to the deeply complex problems which confront our nation in an age of swift change and social upheaval. Under normal circumstances the appeals of demagogues have attraction only to the lunatic fringe. However, during a crisis such as the cold war in which we are now engaged they become a real threat to democracy.

Despite the growing disdain of all thinking Americans, these rabble-rousers continue their vicious crusade. If anything, their activities have increased in intensity and they can no longer be dismissed as cranks. They continue to peddle their poisonous package of defective and dangerous goods, hoodwinking honest but uninformed Americans with the sweet elixir of an easy cure for complex problems. In an effort to delude Americans they call their product conservatism, but it is a contaminated conservatism that would conserve nothing, but would destroy and devour basic democratic institutions.

Curiously, America has always been fertile soil for right-wing radicalism. Side by side with our democratic traditions has run a persistent mistrust of democratic practice. More than 100 years ago the American Party, better known as the Know-Nothing Party, pricked the vulnerable nerve of anti-foreign sentiment. On an anti-Catholic, anti-immigrant platform, the Know-Nothings elected Senators and Representatives in Congress and controlled state governments for several years. Their presidential candidate in 1856, former President

Millard Fillmore, captured one-fifth of the popular vote.

The influence of early American rightist hatemongers has remained in robust good health for a century. Their heirs of the past few decades have been legion. They wore hoods and lynched Negroes as Ku Klux Klan members in the 1920's. They goosestepped among the fascistic Silver Shirts and Fritz Kuhn's German-American bund and joined Father Coughlin's Christian front in the 1930's. Today they read as gospel Gerald L. K. Smith's hate sheet, *The Cross and the Flag*, or have been swept into the John Birch Society, in my opinion the most dangerous organization in the United States today. I regret that it has so many members in my state of Ohio.

There are nearly 1,000 radical right-wing organizations in the nation, many, like Lincoln Rockwell's American Nazi Party, and the Minutemen, number only a few hundred psychopaths and crackbrains each. Others such as Billy James Hargis' Christian Crusade, the Manion Forum, the National Economic Council, Fred Schwarz' Christian Anti-Communist Crusade, Americans for Constitutional Action, and Young Americans for Freedom are larger, well financed, and reach millions of Americans through their propaganda and radio and television programs. Many of them regularly distribute massive quantities of wildly irresponsible literature, some of which comes to me in the mail directly and attached to letters from constituents. I know that many of my colleagues receive the same or similar hate pamphlets. Earlier this year, the distinguished senior Senator from California [Mr. Kuchel] discussed at length in this chamber his experience in this regard.

Who are the people who believe this propaganda? They are the frightened and the frustrated; the bitter and the vindictive; the twisted zealots and well-meaning cranks; the malicious cynics and confused innocents; the people who have nightmarish fears of a radical bogey, who suspect eggheads, who hated and still hate the New Deal or who hate anyone who differs with their extremist views.

Who are the leaders of the radical right-wing groups? Many are sincere believers in their causes of hate. Others typified by Robert Welch, founder and fuehrer of the John Birch Society, are cold opportunists who have carved lucrative careers by playing on the prejudices of their adherents.

Some years ago, when Welch ran for the nomination for Lieutenant Governor of the state of Massachusetts, he did not even make a respectable showing. Welch and hatemongers such as Fred Charles Schwarz, Gerald L. K. Smith, Billy James Hargis, Kent and Phoebe Courtney, and others have discovered that spreading their messages of hate and utterly false accusations can be a very profitable occupation, indeed. Schwarz grossed $1,250,000 in 1961 and close to a million dollars in 1962. Life membership in the John Birch Society can be bought for the "bargain price" of $1,000. Welch has made it quite clear that he is not to be held accountable for his use of these funds. The number of members and the manner in which their membership dues are expended need never be divulged. Cell meetings of the society are secret.

It is now obvious that there is something akin to an interlocking directorship of the many lunatic right-wing organizations. Each can no longer be dismissed as just another group of crackpots or fortune hunters. Careful study of right-wing activity reveals that there is constant communication between these groups and that many leaders are either active members or contributors to a whole raft of these organizations. Birchites sit on the national advisory board of "We, the People," a Hargis enterprise. The head of the California Free Enterprise Association served on Hargis' Christian Crusade and on the steering commmittee of a Fred Schwarz School of anti-Communism, and so on ad infinitum, or perhaps I should say ad nauseam.

Under the guise of jousting with alleged Communists, these groups undermine our basic institutions and try to reshape America into a totalitarian–fascist state. Their tactics are the big lie and the wanton smear.

Unable to impeach Chief Justice Warren, or convince Americans that former President Eisenhower is a conscious tool of the Communist conspiracy, they are willing to settle, temporarily, for the head of a schoolteacher in California, a clergyman in Texas, or a state legislator in Wyoming. The medicine men of the right sell their followers the diagnosis that internal communism is the disease which causes all ills, and then prescribe local vigilante action as the cure. I do not like people who seek to play God with other people's patriotism.

A Communist, as far as the Birchites and their cohorts are concerned, means anybody who approves of the necessity of paying income taxes, public education, publicly owned post offices, civil rights, the United Nations, labor unions, and so on. Their creed must please the Soviet and Chinese Communists no end, for its essence is a form of unilateral disarmament through the decay of vital national services which would drastically weaken our country, a breakup of federal authority, and a withdrawal from the international field.

Any American who disagrees with or disputes the dogma of these demagogues of the right is automatically subject to suspicion. In the name of freedom they would stifle debate, smother ideas, and muzzle the American people.

In states such as Wyoming, where right-wingers have recently been particularly active, professors have refused to speak at a seminar to discuss the right-wing movement for fear of losing their jobs. Teachers in our public schools are known to steer away from discussion of even mildly controversial issues for the same reason. In another state, a radio station operator who had expressed anti-Birch sentiment was subsequently forced to close his operation. Right-wing pressure had caused his advertisers to withdraw their business.

This kind of economic intimidation is the most powerful and the most insidious weapon at the disposal of the Birchites. It makes a mockery of the First Amendment. It makes a sham of democracy. It makes livelihood the price of liberty. Most of the debris of the witch-hunts of the early 1950's has been cleaned up, but it is apparent that some of this rubbish still remains.

If Khrushchev and Mao Tse-tung had hired helpers in their announced task of burying us, they could not have chosen better ones than the Birchites and their fellow traveling radical crackbrain followers. They aid and abet the Communists by creating disunity and distrust and undermining our institutions from within.

Mr. President, the majority of Americans are educated, informed, jealous of their rights, and aware of their responsibilities. Our home-grown fascists have been able to pull the wool over only a few eyes. However, the efforts of the Birchites are unceasing and their resources are often unlimited.

One of the newest techniques for bringing their message of hate and fear to Americans is the mobile library. At this moment, John Birch bookmobiles are moving through the streets of our cities and towns, carrying their propaganda to the doorsteps of those who do not seek it out at secret cell meetings. We are all invited to become "acquainted with the truth," as the radical right defines it in statements such as "Democracy is merely a deceptive phrase, a weapon of demogoguery, and a perennial fraud"; "Foreigners are running the country"; "The clergy is riddled with Communists—pull them from their pulpits if necessary."

I know that the vast majority of Americans will not swallow these lies. However, there is the danger that many well-meaning Americans will embrace the easy answers provided by Welch as valid solutions to confusing and complex problems. There is the further danger that the rest of us will not care enough or be sufficiently aware of the threat from the right to present our opposing views with equal vigor and determination. An organized and vocal minority can, indeed, overcome an unconcerned majority. Unfortunately, we have witnessed this occurring time after time during this century in countries throughout the world.

When I express my conviction that the John Birch Society is the most dangerous organization in America, I perhaps give it an importance it does not merit. I do not think so.

The John Birch Society has introduced a new intelligence to the lunatic fringe by developing a formal structure more sophisticated than any other right-wing group. It has evolved secretive community-level cells, just as the Communists did. Its leader—its "little Hitler"—Robert Welch, maintains rigid control of programs and activities. Because of its secret nature, the society has drawn into its ranks and into its leadership ultra-respectable business and industrial leaders who shun participation in the more clamorous right-wing groups. They have money and influence and are willing to use both for the organization. The monetary support of these business leaders, plus that of the ordinary John Birch Society members, brings the society an estimated income of more than $1,500,000 a year. Since its founding in 1958 the society is believed to have attracted more than 60,000 members.

Mr. President, America has enough headaches in finding a course of action to meet the encroachments and challenges of international communism and Soviet and Red Chinese imperialism. We do not need the radical right to complicate matters. Every picture of a race riot, North or South, fomented by right-wing extremists, every American smeared by fellow Americans for his political beliefs, every reckless charge against responsible government officials by the demagogues of the right does more to serve the aims of international communism than 5,000 American Communists could hope to do.

Speaking of the radical right, J. Edgar Hoover, warned that—

> Attributing every adversity to communism is not only irrational but contributes to hysteria and fosters groundless fears. . . . The way to fight it is to study it, understand it. . . . This is neither the time for inaction nor vigilante action.

I am reminded that Dr. Hutchins, when chancellor of the University of Chicago, was asked by a right-wing lady, "Dr. Hutchins, do you really teach communism in the University of Chicago?"

He said, "Yes, lady; and we also teach cancer in our medical school."

There is plenty of room in the United States for responsible conservatism. What a dull country it would be if we were all progressives and liberals. However, the groups I have described, and the vicious methods they employ, are irresponsible and destructive.

They do not grow because of the attractiveness of their aims. Few Americans would choose fascism over democracy. They grow because of the unawareness, the apathy, and the fear of many Americans. Too many may laugh or shrug these rabble-rousers off as mere mischief-makers or annoyances. Too many may remain unaware of the proposals which they push through state legislatures and of the lies which they spread. Too many may ignore the economic weapons which they wield. Meanwhile, these self-appointed vigilantes are hard at work.

Mr. President, unfortunately today all American taxpayers are indirectly financing many of thse vicious organizations. Although our laws do not grant tax-exempt status to an organization, a substantial part of whose activities is carrying on propaganda, there is increasing evidence, as the distinguished junior Senator from Oregon [Mrs. Neuberger] has pointed out, that dozens of these groups are masquerading as educational and religious organizations, flooding the country with partisan political propaganda, and are financed by tax-free contributions from businessmen.

Unfortunately some of these contributors are also retired and soft-brained generals and admirals. In 1961 a score or more of these lunatic right-wing-oriented propaganda organizations took in more than $5.5 million in tax-free contributions.

Mr. President, how is it that such a flagrant abuse of the charitable deduction provisions of the income tax law is permitted to exist? What justification do Internal Revenue Service officials give for allowing this situation to continue?

I do not propose that committees of Congress caravan about the country conducting investigations into the activities of the radical right. I believe we have had enough investigations into the political beliefs of free American citizens. However, I do propose that corrective action be taken to close this tax loophole favoring these book-burners and witch-hunters.

It is time to put an end to this tax loophole; and I hope that this will be done later, when tax legislation is considered.

Mr. President, the radicals of the extreme right are at odds with the very purpose of our nation—freedom and democracy. If they are to be restrained and to be prevented from giving further solace and comfort to our Communist adversaries, they must be subjected to constant exposure and relentless publicity. We must continue to show them as the demagogues they are. America is last with them.

Let the American People Beware*

Senator Lee Metcalf

Though it was not possible to show it through quotations in the chapter, "The Extreme Right Views the World," one of the characteristics of extremist writings today is a concern with scholarly trappings. Thus Robert Welch's 300-page work on Eisenhower, *The Politician,* is followed by more than 100 pages of bibliography and footnotes. Many of the references in rightist works are to other people on the right and to certain government documents, often publications of the House Committee on Un-American Activities. At various times commentators have dissected rightist works and have found some of the scholarship to be spurious, full of excerpts from nonexistent reports, references to publications that have nothing to do with the subject, quotations that turn out to be bogus. In the following speech, Democratic Senator Lee Metcalf of Montana tells of his vain attempt to track down the source of a single alleged quotation.

A basic maxim of law is *falsus in uno, falsus in omnibus.* A witness' testimony, if false as to any material part, generally should be discarded as a whole and cannot be relied on for any purpose, unless strongly corroborated.

One of the statements thrown at members of Congress many times in recent months reads as follows:

> We cannot expect the Americans to jump from capitalism to communism, but we can assist their elected leaders in giving Americans small doses of socialism, until they suddenly awake to find they have communism.

The quotation is attributed to Nikita Khrushchev, and is said, by the people who use it, to have been made some three and a half months before his visit to the United States in September, 1959.

I have seen this statement in letters to editors. It is sometimes attached to letters I receive. Sometimes it is printed, against a red background, on postcards distributed as a public service by Coast Federal Savings of Los Angeles, which has circulated thousands of copies of literature endorsing the John Birch Society.

Sometimes it appears on postcards bearing the imprint of Poor Richard's Book Shop of Los Angeles, which disseminates right-wing

---

*Congressional Record, 87th Congress, Sess. II, p. 3676.

material. Sometimes, in mail I receive, this quotation is followed by statements like the following: "Your socialistic voting record leads me to believe that you are one of the elected leaders upon whom Nikita Khrushchev depends to carry out his plan."

I asked the Library of Congress to find the origin of the statement. I received the following reply:

> We have searched the Legislative Reference Service files, checked all the standard reference works on quotations by Khrushchev, and consulted with the Slavic Division of the Library of Congress, the Department of State, and the U.S. Information Agency, in an attempt to determine the authenticity of this quotation. From none of these sources were we able to produce evidence that Khrushchev actually made such a statement.

I asked the Senate Internal Security Subcommittee if its files showed any documentation for the quotation. Chairman James O. Eastland, on February 26, advised me that: "Inquiry to the Slavic Division of the Library of Congress discloses no authentic source for the quotation."

A similar inquiry to the House Committee on Un-American Activities brought the following response, dated March 2, from Chairman Francis E. Walter: "The research section of our committee as well as the Legislative Reference Service of the Library of Congress have been unable to find the origin of the quotation referred to above."

I queried Director J. Edgar Hoover of the Federal Bureau of Investigation. On March 1, he advised me that: "I have had the files and reference material available to us reviewed; however, it has not been possible to verify the authenticity of the statement."

I asked the Central Intelligence Agency. On February 13, 1962, Director John A. McCone advised me as follows:

> The quotation ... does not appear in any of Khrushchev's speeches, interviews, articles, or off-the-cuff remarks which have come to our attention. To the best of our knowledge, we believe the quotation to be spurious.

Mr. President, this fabrication, attributed to the leader of the Communist Party, arouses Americans against their elected officials. Readers and listeners are led, by the mischievous persons who authored and use the false quotation, to believe that their President, their Senators, their Representatives, their judges and local officials are Communist stooges. Thus a lie is used to perpetrate a greater lie.

I say, Mr. President, that whoever created this quotation, and those who, knowing it to be spurious, nevertheless disseminate it, are cut from the same cloth as Communists and fascists. Totalitarian movements always strive to belittle and subvert democratic or republican government. Let the American people beware.

Peril to Conservatives*

In the following editorial, which appeared at the end of a series of articles in the *Los Angeles Times* on the John Birch Society (March 12, 1961), Publisher Otis Chandler said that conservatives, though wholeheartedly against communism, must eschew the methods of the John Birch Society. Though directed only at that organization, the editorial obviously condemns many positions and practices common to the extreme right.

The *Times* published last week a heavily documented series of articles which defined the nature and methods of the John Birch Society in the words of its absolute master.

The quotations from Robert Welch, and from some of his lieutenants, nail down the treacherous fallacy that an honorable or noble objective justifies any means to achieve it.

Our fear of the John Birch Society is based on our own findings, on the meticulously researched articles written by Gene Blake. In them it can be read, within quotation marks, that Communists must be fought with their own weapons, smear for smear. Even—and the quotations are brutal—with sedition.

Every conservative must adhere to the general purpose of the society as it is stated by Robert Welch: "to promote less government more responsibility and a better world."

Every loyal American must agree devoutly with the society's immediate intention of "stopping the Communists and destroying their conspiracy, or at least breaking its grip on our government and shattering its power within the United States."

And every informed American must agree with the society's tenet that the United States is actually now engaged with Soviet Russia in a struggle for the survival of our system.

With all honorable Americans, this newspaper looks with disgust and dread upon the godless materialism and blood-soaked tyranny of the Communist conspiracy. It is because of our people's disgust and

---

*Reprinted from *Congressional Record*, 87th Congress, Sess. I, pp. 4268–9, with the permission of the *Los Angeles Times*.

dread that the Communists must seek their ends by secret subversion, by seducing officials, by discrediting our institutions, sowing distrust among us, aggravating union and racial disputes, entering without conscience into any course that will serve the purpose of Moscow.

Then what is likely to happen to the member of the John Birch Society who abandons all the rules by which he has lived his decent life, and adopts instead the techniques and the rules of conspiracy to fight Communists in Communist fashion?

If the John Birchers follow the program of their leader, they will bring our institutions into question exactly as the Communists try to do. They will sow distrust, and aggravate disputes, and they will weaken the very strong case for conservatism.

What are we to think when our last three presidents, Roosevelt, Truman, and Eisenhower, are accused either of being Communists or Communist dupes?

What are we to think when these charges are leveled against Secretary of State John Foster Dulles, against his brother Allen who heads our vital Central Intelligence Agency, against the Chief Justice of our Supreme Court?

What are we to think when the honor and integrity of the Vice-President of the United States, the Republican Party's nominee for president, are questioned?

What are we to think when we are told that our nation's press almost without exception is Communist infiltrated and inspired?

What are we to think when we are told that our churches almost without exception are corroded with active agents of Moscow?

What is happening to us when all loyal Americans are accused of being Communist dupes unless they subscribe to the radical and dictatorial direction of one self-chosen man?

All sincere conservatives must ask themselves these questions. And they must answer them.

The *Times* believes implicitly in the conservative philosophy. It has challenged all these men and most of these institutions on the soundness of one or more issues. But the *Times* does not believe that the argument for conservatism can be won—and we do believe it can be won—by smearing as enemies and traitors those with whom we sometimes disagree.

Subversion, whether of the left or the right, is still subversion.

The John Birch Society*

William F. Buckley, Jr.

For a couple of years after its appearance on the national scene, the Birch Society won the approval of William F. Buckley, Jr., one of the leading conservative intellectuals and publisher of the *National Review*. Eventually disgusted with many of the "paranoid" positions he found Robert Welch taking, he attempted to find out whether the rank-and-file members agreed with their leader. To his dismay, Buckley found they did. The results of his investigation appeared in three columns he wrote in August, 1965, and they are printed below. Again, although the attack is only on the Birch Society, it can be seen that the positions Buckley takes issue with are common to much of the extreme right.

The Birch Society, August 1965

The Birch Society is engaged in a nationwide drive to convince the skeptics of its respectability. Thousands of members of the John Birch Society, who joined it eagerly as a fighting organization devoted to anti-socialism and anti-Communism, have been saying for years that the unfortunate conclusions drawn by Mr. Robert Welch about Dwight Eisenhower in 1958 are altogether extraneous to the Society's mandate, purposes, and mode of thought, and should therefore be ignored in assessing the Society, A.D. 1965.

I regret to say that it is in my judgment impossible to defend the leadership of the John Birch Society if one reads closely even its contemporary utterances. I should like to know how those members of the Society who believe that it long since departed from the mania of Mr. Welch's conclusions about Dwight Eisenhower can justify the current issue of *American Opinion*, the Society's monthly magazine, with its featured article about the extent ("60–80 per cent") of Communist influence in the United States (and elsewhere).

It is an unsigned, staff-written article, given especial prominence. And the editor calls attention to it on the masthead page: " . . . if you want to know what is going on in the world, we strongly recommend the next 144 pages to help you find out."

---

*National Review (Oct. 19, 1965), 916–918. The three columns appeared as headed here, with notices indicating their prior release on August 5, 17, and 21, 1965, in that order. Copyright by the *National Review*, 150 East 35th St., New York, N.Y. 10016.

Mental health? "The attention of the American people was first drawn to the real problem of 'mental health' on October 1, 1962, when, in obedience to the specific demands of the Communist Party, a gang under the direction of Nicholas Katzenbach (now Attorney General of the U.S.) kidnaped General Edwin A. Walker in Oxford, Mississippi. . . ."

Medicare? " . . . the principal object of 'Medicare' is to destroy the independence and integrity of American physicians. . . . It will inevitably create a 'pressing shortage' of physicians and nurses. Communist provinces are sure to have a surplus . . . they will be glad to export to the United States to relieve the shortage."

The death of Kennedy? " . . . The Communists were able to exploit their assassination of Kennedy." ("It is gossip in Washington that Earl Warren succeeded in destroying all copies of the pertinent part of a motion-picture film which showed who escorted Jack Ruby through the police lines so that he could silence Oswald.")

Civil Rights? Selma: " . . . a horde of termites from all over the country, led by half-crazed ministers and professors, swarmed over the small town of Selma, Alabama, in a typical demonstration of Communist activism." The Civil Rights Act of 1964: "[It was a] part of the pattern for the Communist takeover of America." In general: " . . . [it is] an obvious fact that the whole racial agitation was designed and is directed by the international Communist conspiracy."

The economic situation? "The conspiracy can now produce a total economic collapse any time that it decides to pull the chain."

The lower courts? " . . . do not overlook the fine contributions made by the criminals whom the conspiracy has slipped into lower courts."

The Supreme Court? "The theory that the Warren Court is working for a domestic, as distinct from foreign, dictatorship becomes less tenable every day."

The federal government? "Communist domination of many of the departments of the Federal Government is too obvious to require much comment."

Foreign policy? "As for Vietnam, one thing is certain: no action really detrimental to the Communists is conceivable or even possible, so long as Rusk, McNamara, and Katzenbach remain in power."

The Dominican Republic? " . . . the policy that began with the landing of Marines in Santo Domingo [came] under the direction of what often seems to be Communist headquarters in Washington—officially called the State Department."

Summary? "The important point is that Americans can expect only defeat so long as they are commanded by their enemies."

One continues to wonder how it is that the membership of the John

Birch Society tolerates such paranoid and unpatriotic drivel. Until the members rise up and demand a leadership whose programs and analyses are based other than on the premise that practically every Liberal politician, every confused professor, every civil rights demonstrator, every ideologized judge, every bungling diplomat, every avid prosecutor, everyone who wants free medicine, and civil rights legislation, and government control of the economy, is an agent of the Communist conspiracy—until then, at least, they oughtn't to go about the country complaining that the Society is consistently misrepresented. But their views aren't the Voice of the John Birch Society. That Voice you have just heard.

More on the Birch Society

One week ago I wrote a column expressing a dismay I felt sure was shared by the majority of the members of the John Birch Society at some of the positions being subtly advanced by the leadership of the JBS in its magazine, *American Opinion*, even while the Society is spending tons of dough to appease public opinion and persuade the average American that the leadership is non-kooky. The response has been discouraging to those who (like myself) have steadfastly adhered to the position that between the opinions of Robert Welch and those of his votaries there is a great gulf: that the latter calmly disbelieve, or ignore, his enormities, remaining loyal to the Society on the grounds that you need simply scrape off the barnacles of extremism and have left a trim seagoing hull bent on an upwind anti-Communist, anti-socialist course.

I am troubled by the initial response to that column, and have decided to extend my inquiry into the nature of the support of the John Birch Society in an effort to answer several questions. One: Is there in fact substantial disagreement between the membership at large, and the leadership of the JBS? Two: Do the members of the JBS make any attempt to understand what it is that the leadership of the JBS believes; or do they simply ignore the zanier findings of the leadership, taking shelter in the argument that the Society is anti-Communist, and that therefore all anti-Communists should support it?

Mr. Robert Welch, the founder of the John Birch Society, has often expressed his pride in the character and gentility of his members. I say it sincerely that I do not doubt that he is to a considerable extent correct. But I also doubt, to judge from the response to date, that he could easily explain away the manners of some of the more vociferous members of his Society.

Mr. William Patten of St. Louis, Mo., for instance, suspects my motives. "So, The Establishment has finally gotten to you! The word is Comply—or else! Or else what? Your magazine will not be distributed by 'accepted' distributors! Cancel My Subscription" (hereinafter, CMS). Mrs. Lenore McDonald of Los Angeles: "What Robert Welch wrote in *The Politician* (imputing pro-Communism to Dwight Eisenhower) is mild."

Mrs. W. D. Porter of Lexington: "Did you just have to do it? Couldn't you have left it to the Overstreets, Gus Hall, and perhaps Chet Huntley? CMS." Mr. William Gehrke of Denver, Colo.: "The same old smear method employed by the Liberals is used, namely, condemn the man and what he stands for but don't dare try to refute his facts [*i.e.*, that the United States is 60-80 per cent dominated by Communists, that being the conclusion of the article I quoted]. CMS."

Mrs. George Caldwell of San Crescento, Calif.: "Since I have just so much hate in me I must parcel it out rather sparingly, and as I understand you I am now to love Russia and hate the John Birch Society." Mrs. R. S. Matthews of New York: "One more thing before you open your big mouth again, ask Congress to give a hearing to Col. Goliewski." (Who will *prove* that Ike is a Communist?) Mrs. Monica Doeing of Santa Barbara, Calif.: "Do you mean that you *don't* think that the kidnaping of General Walker was a part of the Communist conspiracy? If so, you better get your head out of the sand."

Mr. and Mrs. John Dalziel of Brooklyn: "When you attack Robert Welch you attack every member in the Society." Mr. Arthur Barksdale of San Mateo, Calif.: "I have always believed you to be a true conservative. However, since you seem categorically to accept most of the left-wing programs I'm beginning to doubt your sincerity."

Mr. Robert Jonas of Oyster Bay, L.I.: "I am unable to understand whether in this latest attack, you are just being officious, or whether you periodically suffer from hot flashes, in some form of male menopause? CMS." Mr. James Oviatt of Los Angeles and Beverly Hills: "I am just wondering what Zionist Jew wrote this article? Could it have been Lippmann, Goldberg, or even Abe—Johnson's attorney? . . . I have known Bob Welch for over fifteen years; I think he told the truth about Eisenhower."

Miss Patricia Huster of Baltimore, Md.: "I believe I heard that there was some $95,000 involved in your last smear of the John Birch Society. How much did you get paid this time? And by the way, whose side are you on, anyway? CMS." Mr. Lee Adamson of Bellingham, Wash.: "I have heard a rumor that John Kenneth Galbraith is a majority stockholder in *National Review*."

And Mr. J. T. Timothy of Willimantic, Conn., sums it up in a single word, in large red crayon: "Judas!"

And Finally on John Birch

I have labored to find the answer to the question: does the typical member of the John Birch Society wince when the leadership makes spectacular remarks imputing pro-Communism to the highest officials of government? I have received 200 (and they continue to pour in) letters since I quoted in this column from an article in the current issue of Mr. Welch's magazine, *American Opinion*. Of those 200 correspondents, only two (2) joined me in deploring the article's excesses.[1]

I quoted some typical reactions in an intermediate column. Today I quote from Mr. Frank Cullen Brophy of Phoenix, Arizona, whose distinguished career as a gentleman, banker, rancher, and writer is well known in the Southwest. He is a member of the National Council of the John Birch Society. Let us see how his mind reacts on the questions at issue.

I quoted from the *American Opinion* article the following sentence: "The attention of the American people was first drawn to the real problem of mental health on October 1, 1962, when, in obedience to the specific demands of the Communist Party, a gang under the direction of Nicholas Katzenbach (now Attorney General of the U.S.) kidnaped General Edwin A. Walker in Oxford, Mississippi."

Whereupon Mr. Brophy writes me: "General Walker *was* kidnaped, or at least seized unlawfully, confined in a mental institution or prison without proper medical examination, and after some days released due to the patriotic pressures of thousands of outraged Americans. The oddest thing about this is that you think it odd that the John Birch Society takes a dim view of such totalitarian tactics and tries to arouse people before it is too late."

Here, preserved in formaldehyde, is a specimen of the utter hopelessness of communication with anyone suffering from advanced Birchitis. I happen to agree with every syllable of Mr. Brophy's dismay at what was done to General Walker, and am abundantly on record to that effect. But the operative words in the Birch article were that Walker was detained *"in obedience to the specific demands of the Communist Party"*—words to which Mr. Brophy does not even bother to allude!

---

[1] The current count is 600 letters, of which about 50 express misgivings over Mr. Welch's statements.

Again, I had quoted *American Opinion:* "The theory that the Warren Court is working for a domestic, as distinct from foreign dictatorship, becomes less tenable every day."

Mr. Brophy writes me, by way of justification: "The pro-Communist activities of the Court in recent years are so obvious that I find it hard to believe that you would find any comment to offer."

The vital difference between *pro-Communism in effect* and *pro-Communist in intention* it once again does not cross Mr. Brophy's mind to mention. When J. Edgar Hoover, by relaxing his vigilance, permitted several convicted members of the Communist Party to slip off to Mexico, the result was pro-Communist in effect; but hardly by design. When the Founding Fathers ratified the First Amendment to the Constitution, they committed an act that was profoundly pro-Jacobin, and ultimately pro-Communist, in effect; but was hardly such by design. When the Warren Court interprets that First Amendment in such a way as to grant license to the Communist Party, it is most certainly doing something that is pro-Communist in effect, but in the absence of evidence that the justices are secret friends of the Communist conspiracy, hardly pro-Communist by design. One can deplore, as for instance Professor Sidney Hook (and I) have done, the absolutization of the First Amendment in such fashion as to help conspirators, without questioning the motives—as distinguished from the judgment—of the ideologues on the Court.

And besides, the Birch article suggests in plain English that the Warren Court is "working for," i.e., is hoping to bring into being, "a foreign dictatorship," which is to suggest, pure and simple, that the majority of the Court are pro-Communist traitors.

Why are such elementary distinctions lost on Mr. Brophy? And on other members of the National Council of the John Birch Society? Hasn't their position, to judge from Mr. Brophy's analysis, clearly come down to the following propositions: (1) Things are going poorly for the United States these days. (2) The reason why is because the people who are running things are Communists and Communist sympathizers. (3) Anyone who believes in Proposition (1) yet cavils at the derivative Proposition (2) is either (a) naive, or (b) irrelevant; and in any event, (c) a clear and present nuisance.

In the absence of public disavowals of this reasoning from responsible members of the John Birch Society, one must henceforward conclude that the minority who object to imputing pro-Communism to such as Attorney General Katzenbach, and to Justices Warren, Black, Douglas and Brennan, are overruled; that the majority of the members of the Society sanction the imputation of treasonable motives to such men as these, not to mention Dean Rusk, Allen Dulles, Robert McNamara, etc., etc.

Mrs. Michael Vaccariello of Glendale, California, writes me: "I have often quoted your sentence [in *Up From Liberalism*, decrying the Liberals' toleration of some of Mrs. Roosevelt's enormities during the forties and fifties]: 'The intellectual probity of a person is measured not merely by what comes out of him, but by what he puts up with from others.' It seems to me, having written that and then having read that issue of *American Opinion*, you could only have written what you did—to have remained silent would not have been discreet, but debasing." Mrs. Vaccariello is a member of the John Birch Society. She appears, alas, to be hopelessly outnumbered.

Vigilantes Not Needed

J. Edgar Hoover

As a nonpartisan appointee, FBI Director J. Edgar Hoover should perhaps not be put in a section devoted to the conservative reaction to the far right. However, the right itself considers Hoover a true conservative, perhaps the only government official really concerned about and attempting to cope with the communist menace. Often, rightist publications will quote Hoover's pronouncements on communism. What they never quote are the FBI chief's statements about vigilante anti-communism. Though he never refers to the extreme right by name, there can be little doubt that Hoover has the right in mind in the following excerpts.

Shall It Be Law or Tyranny

Our fight against communism must be a sane, rational understanding of the facts. Emotional outbursts, extravagant name-calling, gross exaggerations hinder our efforts. We must remember that many noncommunists may legitimately on their own oppose the same laws or take positions on issues of the day which are also held by the communists. Their opinions—though temporarily coinciding with the Party line—do not make them communists. Not at all. We must be very careful with our facts and not brand as communist any individual whose opinion may be different from our own. Freedom of dissent is a great heritage of America which we must treasure.

Today far too many self-styled experts on communism are plying the highways of America giving erroneous and distorted information. This causes hysteria, false alarms, misplaced apprehension by many of our citizens. We need enlightenment about communism—but this information must be factual, accurate and not tailored to echo personal idiosyncrasies. To quote an old aphorism, we need more light and less heat.*

No Vigilantes

There exists today in our land a vital "rift" which the communists are exploiting. Unfortunately, this involves certain people across the country who engage in reckless charges against one another. The label "communist" is too often indiscriminately attached to those whose views differ from the majority. Those whose lives are not led according to what one segment of society might decree to be the "norm" are too frequently challenged as "Reds."

Attributing every adversity to Communism is not only irrational, but contributes to hysteria and fosters groundless fears. . . .

The job of curtailing and containing communism is one for legally constituted authorities with the steadfast cooperation of every loyal citizen. This is neither the time for inaction nor vigilante action.†

The Communist Party Line

In itself, each of the immediate demands proposed by the [Communist] party may be entirely legitimate, or even popular, in nature, representing a desire for a limited and specific reform within the framework of our present system of government. Very frequently, these demands do not originate with the Communists at all but in wholly non-Communist segments of the population.

Because Communism thrives on turmoil, the party is continuously attempting to exploit all grievances—real or imagined—for its own tactical purposes. It is, therefore, almost inevitable that, on many issues, the party line will coincide with the position of many non-Communists. The danger of indiscriminately alleging that someone is a Communist merely because his views on a particular issue happen to

---

*American Bar Association Journal, XVIII (February, 1962), 120.

†Law Enforcement Bulletin (April, 1961), 2.

parallel the official party line is obvious. The confusion which is thereby created helps the Communists by diffusing the forces of their opponents.

Unfortunately, there are those who make the very mistake the Communists are so careful to avoid. These individuals concentrate on the negative rather than the positive. They are merely against Communism without being for any positive measure to eliminate the social, political or economic frictions which the Communists are so adroit at exploiting.

These persons would do well to recall a recent lesson from history. Both Hitler and Mussolini were against Communism. However, it was by what they stood for, not against, that history has judged them.†

---

†The Communist Party Line, prepared by J. Edgar Hoover, Senate Document No. 59, 87th Congress, Sess. I (Washington: Government Printing Office, 1961), pp. 5–6.

Chapter Five

The Extreme Right in Perspective

To the historian the extreme right is far too recent a phenomenon to be seen in the kind of perspective that he desires for evaluating significance. The social scientist is also handicapped in studying this problem because members of the academic profession are for the most part distrusted by extremists, who often see the "academic establishment" as a kind of communist front. Thus, for the most part it is difficult to obtain interviews with or have questionnaires filled out by extreme rightists, and social scientists are deprived of much of the information they need for analyzing social groups.

None of these drawbacks, however, have kept academicians from studying the extremists. Sociologists, political scientists, psychologists and historians have broken into print with analyses of the social, historical and ideological backgrounds of the rightists. None of their explanations can in any way be considered definitive, and quarrels over the problem will undoubtedly rage for decades. Yet many of these analyses are both provocative and suggestive, and most of them undoubtedly supply at least a little piece of a very complex truth. The articles in this section do no more than give a brief introduction to the kinds of things scholars have been saying about the right. Students interested in pursuing the topic further should consult the Suggestions for Further Reading.

The Radical Right*

Eugene V. Schneider

One of the curious things about protest from the right is that unlike left-wing radicalism, which tends to arise in times of economic crisis and deprivation, it has been fostered in a period of prosperity and increasing affluence. Some social scientists explain this by drawing a distinction between "class politics," which occur in depression eras and in which radicalism flourishes around bread-and-butter issues, and "status politics," which occur in prosperous periods when various social groups, well-off enough financially, are likely to become concerned about their relative status in the nation. Though he does not explicitly use these terms, sociologist Eugene Schneider shows in the following article how, in spite of prosperity, certain social groups are in a state of crisis today, and that because of this they furnish recruits for the far right. He also puts forth the original idea that the anti-communism of the right is related to a general anti-communism of almost all Americans, including liberals. For Schneider, the whole society is suffering from something he calls "ahistoricism."

In spite of optimistic predictions following the demise of McCarthyism, the voice of the right-wing radical is heard loud and clear in our land once more. Of course, it has never been completely silent, but of late it seems to have acquired new decibels. This seems to have come as a surprise to many, who assumed that right-wing radicalism had been all but eliminated, or at least relegated to the fringes of society. How can we account for its persistence, its constant resurgence?

Of one thing we can be sure: right-wing radicalism is endemic in ·industrial–capitalist society at a certain stage of development; there has been no advanced industrial–capitalist society free of it, though it has appeared in varying degrees of effectiveness, virulence and self-consciousness. This would suggest that it is indigenous to our milieu; that, whatever one may think of it, it arises out of the experience of living in modern society. At the same time, one must recognize that each right-wing radicalism—including our own brands—is a response to a particular concatenation of social forces, existing at a special time and undergoing its own process of development.

Whatever social forces are producing this radicalism at a given time, and whatever form it may take, there is a certain unity to its

---

*Nation (Sept. 30, 1961), 199–203.

interpretation of the world and to the remedies it proposes for the world's ills. The essence of right-wing radicalism is a special kind of *ahistoricism*. Speaking generally, and no doubt too hastily, the ahistorical position is that history is without meaning or design; it is the accidental, meandering, aimless result of powerful wills, or chance, or an unchanging human nature. It is not social forces such as the development of economic relations, the progress of technology or science, the concentration of men in cities, the struggles of people for freedom, which are the prime movers of history; it is individual men who make history, and some of them, at any rate, can make it as they choose.

Now, whether one happens to agree or not with this position, it is an intellectually respectable one, and many people who are not right-wing radicals adhere to it, consciously or unconsciously, in one form or other—a point to which we will return. But the right-wing radical interprets this doctrine in a special way. For him it is not really essential to believe in a past course of history (though some doctrines are, no doubt, more compatible to him than others). It is around the present that his ahistoricism is concentrated. The point for the right-wing radical is that the present order of society, or some part of it—its economic institutions (except as they have been distorted and perverted), its property relationships, its class and race structure, or whatever else he cherishes—is the only natural, sane, morally correct, viable order. Whether this has come about as the result of chance, through the acts of great men, or as the result of historical evolution, hardly matters. We have arrived at the millenium, achieved God's Kingdom on Earth, out-utopia'd all Utopias. By the same token, deviation from this Garden of Eden is insane, unnatural and immoral.

But, alas, there are flies in the ointment, and others are buzzing around the bottle. The forces of social change—to alter the metaphor —beat continually on the ramparts, and here and there they have breached the walls; our cities continue to grow, technology and science develop apace, caries are controlled, new forms of art develop, the doctrines of religion alter, new forms of family life emerge, Negroes continue to demand. Change is everywhere, inexorable, enveloping, insidious. But if this society—never mind whether it exists or ever existed—is perfect, then change can only be the result of imperfect men, perverse men, subversive men. In fact, *all* social change (except that which might conceivably benefit the radical himself, and not even always then) is the outcome of chicanery, fraud, propaganda and plot. Instead of conflict between capital and labor, there is a plot of labor leaders or capitalists or Jews. Instead of an upsurge of Negro masses, there is a plot of Negro leaders. Underlying all attempts to find solutions for the intellectual problems of our times—whether it be a new system of education, a search for a new philosophy, or for a new style in art—is a cabal of eggheads and long-hairs. And yet, all of these separate plots are but aspects of a larger plot, world-encompassing, eternal, evil. This master plot—triumph of radical-right thinking—bears the name of Jew, Catholic, communism, the Devil.

This is how the world appears to the right-wing radical. What does he propose to do about it? Of course, the first item on his agenda is to uncover the plot, to expose it for all to see—whether by the Question, investigation by Congressional committee, or denunciation. The stridency of the right-wing radical's tone, the stringency of his measures, fully match, one can be sure, the enormity of the depravity. At any rate, once the Revelation has been made, the society will, presumably, return to its perfect, unchanging state.

Undoubtedly, many right-wing radicals never go beyond this point in their thinking or in their action. But not all of them are so naive. Recognizing that the forces of change cannot be halted merely by exposure and denunciation, these have evolved a plan, or at least an orientation, for the reconstruction of society, and in a way it is a radical plan. Its essence is the creation of a social order which bypasses or diverts or suppresses the social forces which lie at the basis of the social change that the right-wing radical fears and hates, yet without disturbing the institutions which he cherishes. Men of all classes and stations (except, of course, for the plotters) must somehow be united —in common loyalty to a set of ideas, to a leader. Or, perhaps they can be united in common hatred of someone or something. Conceivably the unity could be achieved on the basis of love, as the late Dr. Buchman wished. But since this item seems to be in scarce supply, the basis for unity is more likely to be sought in irrationality, fear, hatred, frustration, aggression, of which there seems to be no dearth. At any rate, in place of a society mar..ed by those divisions and conflicts which breed change, there will be created a homogeneous, mass society, in which men's hopes, thoughts and loyalties will be severed from their social roots. If even this is not enough, then new institutions will be formed, or old ones exalted—a party?, the state?, a church?—which will unite men under a common rubric of loyalties and discipline. This "new institution" is doubly useful, for it can also serve as the instrument for the forcible suppression of historical evolution, even to the point, as Herr Himmler proposed, of breaking up the large cities—those notorious breeding-places of social and intellectual ferment.

Now, there should be no mystery about which groups and individuals might find this doctrine congenial and meaningful. Every group which has suffered more psychological and material loss than gain from the social processes of our society is a potential recruit to right-wing radicalism. Every individual in whom the deprivations and defeats of life have not somehow been compensated for is a potential recruit. The real questions, for a sociologist, are where these groups and individuals are concentrated in society, why our society should produce so many of them, and what social forces predispose them to accept right-wing radical doctrines as an answer to their ills. The reader should note that there is no attempt here at psychological analysis of the individual recruit, whether he be follower, activist or leader.

At the outset, let us beware of the temptation to explain right-wing radicalism as the expression of an all-powerful "ruling class." The matter is more complicated. For one thing, it is not confined to the "ruling class"; it finds its supporters and breeding places among diverse classes, races, religious groups, ethnic groups and organizations. For another thing, it can be shown, I think, that the "ruling class" is divided in its reactions to right-wing radicalism. All the elites, status groups, molders of public opinion, heads of organizations, who make up the "ruling class," may share the right-wing radical's love for the present order of things. Many of them have been willing to use right-wing radicalism as a means to achieve certain ends. But it is also a fact that many of the present social forces in society operate to protect and further the interests of numerous elite groups. Nor would these groups —let us call them the "entrenched elites"—necessarily welcome any radical reordering of society. It is always a question of whether, in such a reordering, the entrenched elites can retain their preeminence, or even their positions, in society. Those who argue for a class interpretation of right-wing radicalism often point to the relationship between Hitler and the "ruling class" of Germany, but in that instance practically all the elites felt threatened by practically all of the social forces in society.

But there are also certain elites that are by no means so dedicated to the present establishment, either because they feel that certain social forces are inimical, or because they feel cut off from the real centers of power and prestige in the country. As Sweezy and Huberman have shown in their essay on the social backing of McCarthyism, one type of elite is made up of the new millionaires whose wealth is so recent that they have not yet been able to breach the central citadels of power. The Southern elites strive to protect their caste-ridden society against the Negro, and at the same time to carry out a program of industrialization without bother from organized labor. Certain elements of the Johnny-come-lately military elite feel that their roles in the present establishment could be improved, though here hostility to liberal institutions is historical and is based on the military orientation to a seamless society as a framework for its operations. Similarly-oriented elites can be found in other institutions—in churches, in government, in education—expressing either a sense of frustration or the institutional ideology. Then there are what may be called the "sub-elites"— the small manufacturer or businessman can serve as an example— who dislike their own relatively minor roles in society, or who feel threatened by the social forces within it. Every community has them. None of these elites and sub-elites are wedded to the present establishment; some of them fear the social forces within it, some would welcome a reordering along radical lines. It is from among these groups that the major backing for right-wing radicalism comes: the bulk of its financial support, its access to mass media, some of the social respectability it has thus far achieved.

But whence comes the social following, the mass support? The question poses difficulties, because at first glance it would seem that large numbers of people have been treated kindly by many of the social forces which have been operating since World War II. Prosperity, though uneven and spasmodic, has been general. It is not engaging in mythology or apologetics to say that incomes have risen for most people, that gains have been made in status and class position. Even the position of the Negro has improved. Why, then, should right-wing radicalism —supposedly the creation of a society in profound crisis—strike a responsive chord among so many people? Or is there some kind of hidden crisis in our society, not expressed in its general level of material well-being?

The answer lies, I think, in this paradoxical fact: while society as a whole is obviously not in a state of crisis, many groups and people within it are. This latter type of desperation has two separate, though interrelated, aspects. Following Durkheim, I might point out first that the process of social rising is also a process of disorientation; goals recede as fast as they are attained, ties to community are constantly broken, the familiar world is fragmented. People suffer from this as surely as they do from an economic depression; there is something of the same sense of loss, of alienation, of isolation, without even the unifying effects along class lines that a depression may have. Right-wing radicalism offers to such people an outlet for their ambivalence of feeling toward the society: a profound attachment to a social order from which they have benefited, mixed with a profound resentment toward it. It also offers to the most alienated the hope of a less complex, less frenetic state-of-things. Let it be noted that this type of alienation is not a class phenomenon; it involves all those, of whatever class, who have been caught up in the great American game of social (and geographical) mobility.

The second aspect to consider is the nature of social mobility in the United States today. The process is so vast and complex that it is extremely difficult to generalize about it, and virtually impossible to describe in any detail. But, using what evidence is at hand, it can be described more as social churning than social rising. It is not a matter of the appearance of new classes, or of the rise to power of old classes; industrial–capitalism has not changed *that* much. Rather, the situation today is one in which sections of the population, drawn from many different areas of society, have been set into motion of varying kinds and directions. Some groups are rising or falling absolutely; some are rising in reference to certain groups, but falling in relation to others. Even standing still may be the equivalent of rising or falling, relative to other groups. Underlying this churning process are economic, technological and social factors. The prosperity of an arms-oriented economy is not spread evenly over the entire population; in this respect capitalism is almost as anarchistic as it ever was. Automation has disrupted the traditional structure of the working class, and the shock is now spreading to the white-collar groups. Urbanization, suburbanization, the rise of the Negro, the continued depopulation of the countryside, the shifts of population from region to region—all these and other factors have contributed to the turbulence.

The result has been that there are numerous groups and individuals in this country who have reason to hate and fear certain social forces, or who are ambivalent in their feelings toward the society. There is the case of the newly-arrived, who fear that their hard-won status may be threatened by the same social forces through which they have risen. There are those who have experienced real defeat or deprivation either through a failure to rise, or a failure to rise fast enough. There are those who have skidded. This, I think, is the source of the feeling of personal crisis which haunts many Americans today. It is forces of this kind which find expression in the man who has increased his income and his status, but who hates the social forces which are threatening to give him a Negro or a Jew for a neighbor. It is these forces which lead to a blind hatred of change, to the conspiratorial view of the world, and so by direct or indirect paths to right-wing radicalism. And again, let it be noted that except at the very top and the very bottom of society, no section of society is immune to this malaise; it is not, primarily, a class phenomenon.

Now, at this point I have to offer, in a sense, a demurrer to the argument of this paper. The question is: can the present virulence, bellicosity and self-confidence of the right-wing radical movement be explained solely in terms of its roots in the social structure? Undoubtedly, the pressure from certain of the forces described above—automation, unemployment, the Negro upsurge—is increasing. It is possible that the tension from the social-churning process is becoming unbearable in certain sections of society. But for all that, right-wing radicalism remains a fringe movement; in numbers, in the quality of the people it attracts, in the exotic quality of its doctrines. Even those for whom it has a natural attraction continue, for the most part, to act within the structure and definitions of the present social order: for instance, in their voting behavior. The present strength of right-wing radicalism arises, I think, from another source: to wit, from its functional relations to the present establishment, not from its opposition to it.

First, right-wing radicalism served as a handy instrument for liquidating the New Deal, and the climate of opinion which that Establishment had generated. It functioned, and still does, as a means of prosecuting the Cold War and maintaining the armaments economy. It has been used, furthermore, to stifle opposition to these policies. It is true that in the process certain harm has been done to the morality and morale of the country, and this, I think, certain elites really deplore —but not quite to the extent of a willingness to lay aside so potent a bludgeon. What these elites—the entrenched ones—would really deplore would be any attempt of the radical right to implement their remedies. The rise and fall of Joseph McCarthy can serve as an object lesson—to the left as an example of what weapons can be used against them, and to the right as an example of what happens to a radical rightist who gets too big for his britches.

In this connection, it may be that one of the causes of the very latest outbreak is the removal of the restraining hand of Eisenhower. Both Eisenhower and Kennedy represent what is in essence—though not in every particular—about the same balance of forces in this country; that is, they are both of, by and for the present establishment. But Eisenhower had more control over the extreme right. In part this may have been because of his great prestige. But, in addition, Eisenhower divided the loyalties of the right radicals and confused their aims; he was in so many ways the exact mirror image of themselves, he personified so neatly the stability, the simplicity, the unity, they were seeking. With his (whatever liberals may think) uncanny ability to communicate with, and get the trust of, the American people, he must have restrained many who were teetering on the brink of right-wing radicalism. It is possible that the retirement of Eisenhower from public office has, in these senses, swelled the numbers and vociferousness of the extreme right recently.

Secondly, if right-wing radicalism is on the attack today it is because it is consonant with the entire climate of opinion generated by the existing establishment. It is not a matter merely of a common antipathy to communism, or a common dedication to the Cold War. It goes beyond that. It is a matter of the degree to which ahistoricism has entered into almost every aspect of modern thought, its literature, its science (notably its social science), its philosophy, even its art. Just as the New Deal establishment created the climate of opinion in which left radicalism could flourish, so this one creates the conditions which give a certain reasonableness even to extreme right thinking, and—even more important—eviscerates the defense against it.

Really to analyze the deeper-lying causes of this universal ahistoricism would be to write the history of this century: the disillusionment with what social development has brought us, the end-result of scientific progress, the devastating effects of Nazism on hope and trust in humanity, the bitter experience with the Soviet version of socialism. But, in addition, this ahistoricism is powerfully reinforced from within the establishment. As I have said, the ahistorical view of things has not triumphed domestically, where the potentialities of development have not by any means been exhausted. Nor does it spring from the prevailing view of other countries in which industrial–capitalism is strong. It arises, rather, from the attempt of today's establishment to interpret what is going on in many of the non-industrial or non-capitalistic nations.

In those countries, comprising an enormous population with great potentialities of wealth and power, social forces are operating which seem directly contrary to the interests and mentality of our establishment. Nor, try as we may, have we had much success in harnessing these forces to our ends, or turning them in a direction congenial to ourselves. The result has been the almost universal tendency in our society to interpret what is happening as the handiwork of evil or perverse men, the outcome of machination, plot and subversion. (Note how this is reversed for the Russians. For them, what is going on in Africa, Asia and Latin America is the result of inevitable historical forces; it is in Western Europe and Japan that they detect the plots of native and American capitalists.) Furthermore, like any right-wing radical, we detect the master plot behind all of these separate plots. Even the solutions offered are of the radical variety: suppression of the hated social forces by violence, or by diverting or bypassing them.

The ahistoricism which this establishment has generated has

emboldened the right-wing radical, even lent him a certain respectability. But it has had an even more insidious effect on those who would normally have formed the core of the opposition to it; and here I am referring primarily to the liberals and the intellectuals, who have accepted some aspect of this ahistorical thinking. A full analysis of the bowdlerization of the liberal and intellectual must await another occasion. Here I should like to point out that by accepting ahistorical thought, the liberal–intellectual grants the premises of right-wing radical thought, weakens his own moral position, and lessens his powers of resistance. Energies that might have been used against the totalitarians of the right are diverted—into self-analysis, into escape, into disgust and despair with the world.

With every worsening of the cold war, with the appearance of each new revolutionary movement abroad, with every increase of social tension at home, the ahistorical view of the world is strengthened, and by that much the voice of the extreme right radical will become bolder and louder. In this sense, right-wing radicalism is not so much the reflection of America today as it is a barometer of its spirit.

The Radical Right and the Rise of the Fundamentalist Minority*

David Danzig

One does not have to go very deeply into the subject of this book to know that in the world of the rightist, God is on the side of militant anti-communism. Many of the organizations and publications have the word "Christian" in their titles, and it is hardly there by accident. What is less apparent but equally true is that the driving force behind many extremist organizations is that certain branch of Protestantism called fundamentalism. Of course, there are Catholics, Jews and non-fundamentalist Protestants active on the right, but the connection with fundamentalism is important enough to warrant its own study. In this 1962 article, David Danzig, Program Director for the American Jewish Committee, explored the relationship between fundamentalism and extremism and showed the many things they have in common.

―――――――――
*Reprinted from *Commentary* (April, 1962), 291–298, by permission; copyright© by the American Jewish Committee.

Early in February of this year a group of leading Protestant ministers and laymen in Dallas, Texas, were invited to form the core of a local chapter of "Christian Citizen," a new national organization whose announced aim is to train Christians in the techniques of practical politics. The founder of Christian Citizen, Mr. Gerri von Frellick (a Denver real estate developer and a Southern Baptist lay leader), spelled out the program of his movement as primarily an educational one whose purpose is to foster Christian principles in the nation's government and to combat "an increasing sense of futility and apathy in America." Qualifications for membership require only that the recruits must "give testimony of their personal experience with Christ" and must "accept the Bible as the infallible word of God." Once having joined, the "Christian Citizen" will be given an extensive training period at the precinct level and then go to work in the political party of his choice. The organization itself, according to von Frellick, will not endorse any candidate or take partisan stands on controversial issues. Appropriate action will be left to the "graduates" who will organize Christians to vote as a bloc and thus "participate effectively in the nation's political life." It is von Frellick's expectation that the movement will eventually become influential enough to "take over a majority of the precincts in this country."

As to actual political objectives, von Frellick has insisted that these are open and unspecified, the ideology of Christian Citizen being that "the democratic process has room for all viewpoints." When questioned about his position on certain key leaders and groups of the much publicized "radical right," von Frellick said that Dr. Fred C. Schwarz's Christian Anti-Communism Crusade was a "terrific" organization and "doing a fabulous job." He also said that the John Birch Society has "made a tremendous contribution to alerting the American people to the problem of Communism." The main difference which the Denver realtor finds between his organization and these others is that they lack "a positive approach"—whereas Christian Citizen can be "a means of launching an offensive in the ideological struggle with Communism."

Behind the vague and pious slogans, then, what we have here is the most recent formation of a cell nucleus in the growing organism of the extreme right. Christian Citizen also offers a particularly clear example of the relation of the more extreme wing of Protestant fundamentalism to the new ultra-conservative movement—a relationship that has frequently been overlooked or scanted by writers in their haste to explain the movement in purely political terms and to find its roots in the same general rightist tendencies that produced the politics of Father Coughlin or of Senator McCarthy or Senator Goldwater, as the case may be. While it is true, of course, that Senator McCarthy is taken by the John Birch Society as its second great martyr, there are some significant differences between McCarthyism and the new radical right—one of the most decisive of which has precisely to do with the connection between this radical right and extreme Protestant fundamentalism.

Fundamentalism, when noticed at all by our popular journals, is usually patronized as a colorful fragment of an older, vanishing way of life. But the truth is that fundamentalism is a growing socio-religious force in America. While its more moderate wing has been attempting to work out a position of "classic orthodoxy" in theology and an over-all *modus vivendi* with liberal Protestantism (particularly of the National Council of Churches variety), its more extreme wing, defined in good part by a belligerent opposition to liberal Protestantism and deep hostility to the NCC, has by no means lost ground. It is only of this latter group that we shall be speaking in the following pages.

Fundamentalism is not a sect or a denomination or a specific church; it is a rigorously orthodox point of view which completely ·denominates some Protestant denominations and has adherents in many others, including even the Episcopal church. Among its basic doctrines are the inerrancy of the Bible, salvation by faith alone, and the pre-millennial return of Christ. On religious questions, it takes a stand against any attempts at revisionism and modernism. This emphasis upon literalness and purity of doctrine makes the fundamentalist look upon pragmatism in the social world with the same suspiciousness and distaste with which he views revisionism in religious doctrine. His commitment to Biblical prophecy, moreover, results in an anti-historicist perspective which readily supports the conspiracy theory of social change. Given all this, and given the association that came to be developed between the "Protestant ethic" and the ideology of 19th-century capitalism, it is not surprising that fundamentalism should always have had a strong disposition to regard the revisions of this ideology (which were partly inspired by Protestant liberals) as the work of heretics and atheistic radicals, infected with and spreading false doctrines in a conspiratorial manner.[1]

In fundamentalist eyes, departures from nineteenth-century capitalism have carried with them the corruption of virtually sanctified socio-

---

[1] In his *History of Fundamentalism*, Stewart Cole speaks of fundamentalism as "the organized determination of conservative churchmen to continue the imperialistic culture of historic Protestantism, within an inhospitable civilization dominated by secular interests and a progressive Christian idealism."

economic doctrines and have consequently helped to undermine the Christian society. Thus, the fundamentalist's apocalyptic conception of the world as strictly divided into the saved and the damned, the forces of good and the forces of evil, has readily lent itself to reactionary political uses. Fundamentalism today supports a super-patriotic Americanism; the conflict with Communism is not one of power blocs but of faiths, part of the unending struggle between God and the devil. The danger of Communism, therefore, is from within—from the corrosion of faith by insidious doctrines. That is to say, by "collectivism"—the modern fundamentalist's secular counterpart of atheism.

The inherently conservative bent of fundamentalism has been further reinforced in America by regional factors. The fundamentalist population has always been located predominantly in the South, the border states, the Middle West, and in several Western states. It was partly as a spokesman for this population that William Jennings Bryan could talk of the East as "enemy territory," and express their economic plight in the fundamentalist imagery of the "cross of gold" speech. In Bryan, as later in Huey Long, the hatred of finance capitalism, or "Wall Street," by a rural population could produce the reforming spirit of Populism without appreciably liberalizing the impacted prejudices of fundamentalist social attitudes. As H. Richard Niebuhr has said:

> The fundamentalist movement was related in some localities to . . . intense racialism or sectionalism. With them it shared antagonism to changes in the mores which the war [World War I] and its consequences, the rise to power of previously submerged immigrant or racial groups and other social processes, brought forth. The political effectiveness of fundamentalism was due in part to this association and *to the support which it gave to political leaders*, who found in it a powerful symbolism representative of the antagonism of political and economic minorities against the eastern or northern urban industrial majority.

The influence of fundamentalist ideas on the political and social life of these regions is seen in the fact that the states in which the movement predominated were the ones that passed—or nearly passed—statutes forbidding the teaching of evolution in the schools and that first enacted prohibition laws. Similarly, fundamentalism's ancient and unregenerate hostility to Catholicism was in good part responsible for the heavy losses which the Democrat Al Smith suffered in 1928 in these regions.

The states that repudiated Darwinism and Al Smith are today prominent among those nineteen that have passed "Right to Work" laws. Since World War I the social base of fundamentalism has shifted markedly, though few political writers have apparently noticed the shift. Its constituency is no longer mainly made up of sharecroppers and poorly educated villagers. Many fundamentalist churches are modern and imposing, financed by wealthy oilmen from Texas and Oklahoma and prosperous farmers in the wheat and corn belts. Rich and influential lay leaders such as J. Howard Pew and von Frellick now make their influence felt in the power structure of the community and state. The fundamentalists also operate a vast network of colleges, training schools, Bible institutions, Bible prophecy conferences, prayer meetings, and study groups. They have many large publishing houses which blanket small towns with conservative tracts and pamphlets. An increase in Protestant orthodoxy has added members to their churches at a more rapid rate than the liberal churches have been able to show. Though still more numerous in the small sects and local churches such as the Pentecostal and Seventh Day Adventists[2] and among the Southern Baptists, the fundamentalists, in some areas, are also found in the Presbyterian and Methodist churches, and to a lesser degree, in the Episcopal and Congregationalist ones. For example, the members of a Congregationalist church in Los Angeles and an Episcopal church in Fort Worth, both cities with powerful fundamentalist traditions, are likely to have a stronger affinity with these traditions than with those practiced by their sister church memberships in the large New England cities.

Population movements, affluence, and mass culture have all, of course, obscured some of the distinct regional features of fundamentalism. But it would be a mistake to view the more prosperous and integrated surfaces of contemporary fundamentalism as indicating any real loss or modification of its identity. Though it has become increasingly middle class, this has not changed its profoundly conservative character, and its vast wealth and growing respectability have mainly served to broaden the base of its traditional antagonism to modern reform capitalism. Its local and regional character has insulated it from the influence of religious pluralism; still mainly Anglo-Saxon, it has preserved—unlike Catholicism and liberal Protestantism—an ethnic homogeneity that shields it from the liberalizing social adjustments invariably created by contending ethnic interests.

---

[2] Many of these small sects are affiliated with the National Association of Evangelicals, which claims a total membership of about ten million.

With the continuing world crisis, fundamentalism is finding a new political relevance for its doctrines and an arena in which it can exert its growing influence. As *Christian Century*, the leading organ of liberal Protestantism, observed recently: "Now the fundamentalists have apparently decided that the time has come to break out of their isolation and to contend for the soul of American Protestantism." A special target of theirs has been the National Council of Churches—the citadel of modern Protestantism. On the whole the attacks have come in the rural areas rather than the large cities, by means of local media rather than national. (One exception was an Air Force manual charging that the National Council of Churches was infiltrated by Communism, which had the effect of driving the Fourth Baptist Church of Wichita, Kansas—the largest local church in the Baptist Convention—to withdraw from the Convention in protest of its affiliation with the Council.) In those regions populated with churches, schools, publishing houses, and study groups that are dominated by fundamentalists, liberal Protestantism has been subjected to an avalanche of bigotry and calumny exceeded in intensity only by the worst period of anti-Catholic propaganda.

In analyzing the motives behind these attacks, Dr. Truman B. Douglas, formerly vice president of the Board of Home Missions of the Congregational Churches, has explained that "what they really want is to silence the witness of the Church *on all social problems and issues.* . . . " That is to say, on all social issues and problems other than Communism. However, as we began by indicating, the fundamentalist mentality and temperament—in the extreme, unregenerate forms that we are discussing in this article—is unable to view the threat of Russian or Chinese Communism in pragmatic and realistic ways. For the fundamentalist mind the great menace of Communism is less in its military power than in its *doctrines*, and the main threat of these doctrines is not that they operate abroad but at home. Like the "papists" of America who, the fundamentalist continues to believe, have never ceased in their insidious and cunningly concealed attempts to undermine the faith and institutions of Protestant America and to deliver the nation up to Rome, the Communists today are everywhere at work disseminating under such subterfuges as "liberalism" and "middle-of-the-road progressivism" the heretical doctrines of collectivism that are poisoning American faith and subverting its social order. Instead of a puissant and pure Christian America marching resolutely toward its apocalyptic encounter with the Soviet anti-Christ, the nation, drugged with false doctrines and blinded by traitorous leaders, is being carried down the road to appeasement and, eventually, capitulation.

It is not surprising to discover, then, that Robert Welch, who has built his organization to fight a conspiracy which numbers President Eisenhower among its members, should have come from a strong fundamentalist background, or that John Birch himself first prepared for his martyrdom in China by being suspended from college because of the extremist zeal of his fundamentalist activities. Much of the affinity of fundamentalism for what is today called the radical right derives from the attempt to wed Protestant zeal and reactionary animus which developed and took shape during the New Deal years. The leader of one such group, the Christian Freedom Foundation, wrote a diatribe which was titled *The Menace of Roosevelt*. During the same period of the middle 1930's, an organization called Spiritual Mobilization was established "to check the trend toward pagan statism." In coming out of their "isolation," as the *Christian Century* puts it, the fundamentalists are not only "competing for the soul of Protestantism" but are also trying to reassert the traditional cultural and political supremacy of conservative Protestantism. Its leaders—men like the Reverend Billy Joe Hargis, the Reverend Fred C. Schwarz, the Reverend James Fifield—are no less aware than the late Senator McCarthy was of the demagogic possibilities inherent in an anti-Communist crusade. But they enjoy an advantage that McCarthy did not have: a massive potential following which is prepared to accept the belief that a restoration of the influence of the old-time religion must be accompanied by a return to the pre-New Deal era of free enterprise and isolationism if the country is to be purged of its disabling doses of collectivism and internationalism. Thus the fundamentalist movement provides both potent political images and popular support to rally other disaffected Americans of different backgrounds who nonetheless feel that they, as well as the nation as a whole, have been losing power, and who are united not only in their hostility to Communism but in their anti-minority, anti-city, anti-labor, and anti-international attitudes.

The election of a Catholic to the Presidency has signalled the change in America from a Protestant nation with a prevailing Anglo-Saxon tradition to a pluralistic nation with a Protestant tradition. The defeats

that the South has been suffering in civil rights mark the demise of
white supremacy in its own sectional stronghold. Given current population trends, increasing urbanization, the organizational growth of
minority groups, these changes are not likely to be reversed. Not long
ago a leading figure in Spiritual Mobilizers, who also heads a large and
wealthy Los Angeles church, articulated part of what the fundamentalist position amounts to in socio-ethnic terms when he reportedly said,
"We are not going to give the city away to the Jews, Negroes, and Mex-
icans." Such cities as Houston, Miami, and Los Angeles were always
fundamentalist strongholds, but the fact that they are now also centers
of rightist politics is at least partly to be explained in terms of local
responses to a growing Catholic minority, a growing Jewish community,
and rapidly increasing Negro or Spanish-speaking minorities.

While the election of Kennedy reflected a decline in bigotry in some
quarters, his campaign stimulated a recrudescence of it in others; and
his career as President is likely to provoke an increase in self-consciousness among our religious communities and a heightened awareness of
their sources of contention—in other words, it is likely to deepen the
pattern of religious pluralism in America even further. The fundamentalists' reaction to the ascendancy of pluralism is double-sided. As
Anglo-Saxon Protestants, in the main, they are reacting to the loss of
the political dominance that came from their majority position. As
fundamentalist Protestants, however, they are a particularly fervent
and committed religious *minority* and one growing in wealth and numbers and ambition. As such, they are behaving more and more like
other important minorities in America—demanding more time and
space in the media, and devoting more energy to organizing their con-
stituencies for social and political action. Whatever else may develop,
it is abundantly clear that the Protestant fundamentalists have now
taken their place among the other distinct groups—the Catholics,
liberal Protestants, Jews, Negroes, and secular humanists—that make
up the pluralistic socio-religious pattern of America.

In trying to convince the community that America's interest will
best be served through their leadership, many fundamentalist religious
and lay leaders have been moving into the seats of power which have
opened on the radical right. Insofar as militant anti-Communism today
has a socio-religious cast, fundamentalism has replaced Catholicism

as the spearhead of the movement.[3] None of this is to say, of course, that the radical right has become identified with the aspirations of a single group—it would hardly have got off the ground if it had. The radical right cuts across all groups in varying degrees, and no doubt there is still a hard core of Catholic McCarthyites who have followed his sanctified image into the radical right movement. Father John F. Cronin, the author of the pamphlet issued last month by the National Catholic Welfare Conference attacking the new "extremists of the right," was indeed quoted by the *New York Times* as saying that "quite a few Catholics" belong to the John Birch Society.

But supporters of Senator McCarthy were, on the whole, a much more variegated and dispersed group than the constituency of the radical right today seems to be. Though many Catholics found in the Senator an expression of their militant anti-Communism, McCarthyism never became a "Catholic movement." It drew the bulk of its support from the traditional "isolationist bloc"—pro-German and anti-British —who had opposed an alliance with Communist Russia against Nazi Germany. McCarthy also had a sizeable following in the large cities, in the national veterans' organizations, and in working-class groups —particularly those with roots in countries now behind the Iron Curtain.

From his famous first speech in Wheeling, West Virginia, McCarthy clearly played up to the minority groups, who were attracted by his hard anti-Communism, which they saw as posing no threat to the economic gains they had made during the New Deal. For the most part, McCarthy managed to attack New Deal liberalism for allowing itself to be infiltrated by Communists, without directly challenging the policies and practices of reformed capitalism that had been achieved by the Democratic coalition and had come to be supported by the middle-of-the-road consensus in America. Seen in historical perspective, McCarthyism was the final phase in the repudiation of our wartime alliance

---

[3] Father Robert A. Graham, among others, has called attention to this change in a recent issue of *America:* "It was not so long ago that Catholics were regarded as the most active foes of Communism. This can no longer be said today. Dr. Fred C. Schwarz's anti-Communism Christian Crusade is of predominantly Baptist inspirations. The National Education Program of Dr. George S. Benson [of the Church of Christ], is another fundamentalist operation. It is no accident that the key centers of the John Birch Society are in the fundamentalist South and Southwest." An even more authoritative indication of the fact that the new radical right does not lean on a predominantly Catholic base is the campaign begun last month by the National Catholic Welfare Conference—the central administrative body of the American Bishops—to discourage participation by Catholics in extreme anti-Communist movements.

with Russia; the charges of treason and disloyalty were aimed venge-
fully by those who had always considered Stalin a greater menace than
Hitler against those who had taken the opposite position and engineered
the alliance with Russia, and who might therefore be held responsible
for the post-war predicaments which had flowed from that alliance.
However, McCarthyism was virtually devoid of social and economic
content as well as religious inspiration, and so lacked stable bases of
local, popular support. With an all but inevitable logic, McCarthy was
forced to play out his role in the national arena where his main concerns
lay. Once his performance there had been discredited by the changes
in international policy that were already in progress when his star
appeared on the horizon, and by his unchecked hostility to the Executive
branch that was now in the hands of his own party, McCarthy collapsed. And with no further issues and grass-roots support which his
followers could exploit, McCarthyism, in effect, collapsed with him.

The radical right, as we have been seeing, is a very different affair,
one with a definite political, economic, and social purpose, and able to
capitalize on the growing power of an important religious group which
has long felt the denial of its rightful share in shaping the policies of
the nation. To be sure, fundamentalist conservatism is today by no
means a monolithic ideology. Even as von Frellick was attempting to
recruit prominent ministers and lay leaders in Dallas for Christian
Citizen, a leader of the Baptist General Convention of Texas was publicly reminding them of the recent recommendation of the Convention
that "Baptists . . . exercise caution when asked to support efforts to
mobilize Christians into a political power." But despite this recommendation, and despite warnings by other Baptists and moderate
fundamentalists, it remains clear that large numbers of fundamentalists *are* being "mobilized" and that their religious and regional conservatism is converting readily into the ideology of the radical right
and swelling the chorus of reactionary and apocalyptic voices in the
land.

The main strength and appeal of fundamentalist conservatism lies
in its nativist nationalism. In the "gray atmosphere" of America's
tense, cautious international power struggle with the Soviet Union in
a nuclear age—an atmosphere made even more troubled by the rise of
the minorities within the society—its program of "Americanism" becomes a way of explaining the nation's loss of supremacy and auton-
omy; it also provides a set of crusading directives for the road to
Armageddon that dispels uncertainty and discharges both national
tensions and local frustrations. On the international scene, it identifies
America's "decline" and the Communist ascendancy with the loss of

the West's four-hundred-year monopoly of power and with the passing of Anglo-Saxon dominance. The immense strengthening of America's world position since the war counts for nothing in the light of our failure to assume the world dominance which Great Britain has relinquished. The shock which followed Sputnik has doubtless helped to bring on the somewhat delayed discovery by certain people in the hinterlands that the American century had been lost, just as the Supreme Court decision on desegregation and the election of Kennedy woke many of the same people to the fact that political power in America was also passing out of their hands.

The appeal of the new nativist nationalism, however, need not remain confined to the rabid—as McCarthyism, being a form of revenge politics, necessarily was. The redistribution of power both abroad and at home has disheartened many moderate people—those who gladly might have settled for less than a monopoly if they could be sure that the Russians (and the Chinese) would do likewise, and who might have accepted the claims of the racial, religious, and ethnic minorities (and of labor), so long as these did not encroach upon their own lives, and so long as their own interests continued to be dominantly represented. Feeling that all of this is no longer the case, the nativist segment of the Protestant population becomes a prey of those who would like to replace the pluralistic orientation which has led America to a precarious coexistence by a doctrinaire, chauvinistic Americanism seeking to achieve a *"Pax Americana."* In Protestant fundamentalism, imbued with nationalist—not unlike the case of pre–World War II German Lutheranism—many formerly moderate people find a powerful rationale and symbolism for this complex of attitudes. The practical program to support the "Americanist" effort in foreign affairs has the further attraction of asking for the abolition of the welfare state, which the Protestants in question see as benefiting mainly the minorities whose rise to prominence has begun to threaten their control within the society and reshape their America in a different image. Thus they are susceptible to a program which, by calling for a return to a nineteenth-century type of capitalism and an end to collaboration with our allies on an equal basis, will bring into power those native groups who can restore their traditional position in the scheme of things. It is on such anxieties and impulses that the radical right has battened.

Whoever has taken the radical right as amounting to nothing more than the fulminations of a few crackpots, or the temporary prominence of the lunatic fringe achieved mainly by publicity, would do well to ponder the matter further. More thought had better be taken, also, by those who have concluded that since the radical right is unlikely to take over America, it can be disregarded as a growing power bloc and a potential influence for harm.

While it is probably true that the new-found strength of reactionary ideas cannot be said to indicate a turn toward conservatism in the population at large, it does seem to indicate that American conservatism is being pulled to the right. This in itself represents a gain for the ultras. But what gives them an even greater potentiality for influence is the fact that they operate at the local and state levels, where a minimum of pressure can exert a maximum of effect, and where there is no necessity for taking the risk of an all-or-nothing gamble—as McCarthy, working at the national level only, was forced to do. This does not mean that the new ultras are interested only in local affairs. On the contrary, as a distinct and now politically self-conscious minority within the pluralistic pattern, they are demanding a greater voice in the shaping of national policy, which they hope to achieve through a strategy of interlocking local pressures. (The effectiveness of such a strategy can be seen from the enormous amount of attention Manager Mitchell attracted through his attack on public welfare programs in the city of Newburgh; a similar attack in Congress would probably have fallen flat.)

So far as foreign policy is concerned, there is even an advantage to the ultras in being an out-of-power faction: they can conduct their programs with wild irresponsibility, blanketing the country with small undercover cells, repressing free discussion, and imposing a doctrinaire conformity. The effect of all this is to reduce the government's opportunities for a flexible handling of delicate problems such as we now face in Germany, in the UN, in Africa. Perhaps most important of all, the ultras make it very difficult for the country to dissociate itself from the imperialism and white supremacy in which the Anglo-Saxon world has figured so prominently in the past. It is ironic, if not yet tragic, that having more or less united the Western world around the belief that the best way to oppose Communism is through the promotion of social reform and the development of international pluralism, America should now be the scene of a nativist movement which would substitute for this idea a belligerent nationalism, one whose socio-religious mystique is not very different from that with which certain European nations recently experimented and in so disastrous a fashion.

The Paranoid Style in American Politics*

Richard Hofstadter

One of the questions often raised about the extreme right asks whether it is a phenomenon unique to our time or one that has had parallels at other periods in the American past. Utilizing the perspective of the historian, Richard Hofstadter—DeWitt Clinton Professor of American History at Columbia University and analyst of social movements—shows how the right has been with us in one form or another for a long, long time. Indeed, Hofstadter suggests that the "paranoid style" of the extremists is not solely an American one, but an international phenomenon that has occurred in various ways and at various times throughout recorded history.

Although American political life has rarely been touched by the most acute varieties of class conflict, it has served again and again as an arena for uncommonly angry minds. Today this fact is most evident on the extreme right wing, which has shown, particularly in the Goldwater movement, how much political leverage can be got out of the animosities and passions of a small minority. Behind such movements there is a style of mind, not always right-wing in its affiliations, that has a long and varied history. I call it the paranoid style simply because no other word adequately evokes the qualities of heated exaggeration, suspiciousness, and conspiratorial fantasy that I have in mind. In using the expression "paranoid style," I am not speaking in a clinical sense, but borrowing a clinical term for other purposes. I have neither the competence nor the desire to classify any figures of the past or present as certifiable lunatics. In fact, the idea of the paranoid style would have little contemporary relevance or historical value if it were applied only to people with profoundly disturbed minds. It is the use of paranoid modes of expression by more or less normal people that makes the phenomenon significant.

. . . .

Of course, the term "paranoid style" is pejorative, and it is meant to be; the paranoid style has a greater affinity for bad causes than good.

---

*Copyright © 1964 by Richard Hofstadter. Abridged with the permission of Alfred A. Knopf, Inc. from Chapter 1 of *The Paranoid Style in American Politics and Other Essays* by Richard Hofstadter.

But nothing entirely prevents a sound program or a sound issue from being advocated in the paranoid style, and it is admittedly impossible to settle the merits of an argument because we think we hear in its presentation the characteristic paranoid accents. Style has to do with the way in which ideas are believed and advocated rather than with the truth or falsity of their content.

. . . .

. . . What interests me here is the possibility of using political rhetoric to get a political pathology. One of the most impressive facts about the paranoid style, in this connection, is that it represents an old and recurrent mode of expression in our public life which has frequently been linked with movements of suspicious discontent and whose content remains much the same even when it is adopted by men of distinctly different purposes. Our experience suggests too that, while it comes in waves of different intensity, it appears to be all but ineradicable.

. . . .

We may begin with a few American examples. Here is Senator McCarthy, speaking in June 1951 about the parlous situations of the United States:

> How can we account for our present situation unless we believe that men high in this government are concerting to deliver us to disaster? This must be the product of a great conspiracy, a conspiracy on a scale so immense as to dwarf any previous such venture in the history of man. A conspiracy of infamy so black that, when it is finally exposed, its principals shall be forever deserving of the maledictions of all honest men. . . . What can be made of this unbroken series of decisions and acts contributing to the strategy of defeat? They cannot be attributed to incompetence. . . . The laws of probability would dictate that part of . . . [the] decisions would serve this country's interest.[1]

Now let us turn back fifty years to a manifesto signed in 1895 by a number of leaders of the Populist Party:

> As early as 1865–66 a conspiracy was entered into between the gold gamblers of Europe and America. . . . For nearly thirty years these conspirators have kept the people quarreling over less important matters, while they have pursued with unrelenting zeal their one central purpose. . . . Every device of treachery, every resource of

---

[1] *Congressional Record*, 82nd Congress, Sess. I (June 14, 1951), p. 6602; for a similar passage, see McCarthy's book *McCarthyism: The Fight for America* (New York: 1952), p. 2.

statecraft, and every artifice known to the secret cabals of the international gold ring are being made use of to deal a blow to the prosperity of the people and the financial and commercial independence
of the country.[2]

Next, a Texas newspaper article of 1855:

... It is a notorious fact that the Monarchs of Europe and the Pope
of Rome are at this very moment plotting our destruction and threatening the extinction of our political, civil, and religious institutions.
We have the best reasons for believing that corruption has found its
way into our Executive Chamber, and that our Executive head is
tainted with the infectious venom of Catholicism. ... The Pope has
recently sent his ambassador of state to this country on a secret
commission, the effect of which is an extraordinary boldness of the
Catholic Church throughout the United States. ... These minions of
the Pope are boldly insulting our Senators; reprimanding our Statesmen; propagating the adulterous union of Church and state; abusing
with foul calumny all governments but Catholic; and spewing out the
bitterest execrations on all Protestantism. The Catholics in the United
States receive from abroad more than $200,000 annually for the
propagation of their creed. Add to this the vast revenue collected
here. ...[3]

. . . .

These quotations, taken from intervals of half a century, give the
keynote of the style of thought. In the history of the United States one
finds it, for example, in the anti-Masonic movement, the nativist and
anti-Catholic movement, in certain spokesmen for abolitionism who
regarded the United States as being in the grip of a slaveholders' conspiracy, in many writers alarmed by Mormonism, in some Greenback
and Populist writers who constructed a great conspiracy of international bankers, in the exposure of a munitions makers' conspiracy of
the First World War, in the popular left-wing press, in the contemporary American right wing, and on both sides of the race controversy
today, among White Citizens Councils and Black Muslims. I do not
propose to try to trace the variations of the paranoid style that can be

---

[2] The manifesto is reprinted in Frank McVey: "The Populist Movement," *Economic
Studies*, I (August, 1896), 201–2; the platform of the Populist Party) for 1892 asserts: "A
vast conspiracy against mankind has been organized on two continents, and it is rapidly
taking possession of the world. If not met and overthrown at once, it forbodes terrible
social convulsions, the destruction of civilization, or the establishment of an absolute
despotism."

[3] Quoted by Sister Paul of the Cross McGrath: *Political Nativism in Texas, 1825–1860*
(Washington: 1930), pp. 114–15, from *Texas State Times* (September 15, 1855).

found in all these movements, but will confine myself to a few leading episodes in our past history in which the style emerged in full and archetypal splendor.

II

A suitable point of departure is the panic that broke out in some quarters at the end of the eighteenth century over the allegedly subversive activities of the Bavarian Illuminati. This panic, which came with the general Western reaction to the French Revolution, was heightened here by the response of certain reactionaries, mostly in New England and among the established clergy, to the rise of Jeffersonian democracy. Illumism had been founded in 1776 by Adam Weishaupt, a professor of law at the University of Ingolstadt. Its teachings today seem to be no more than another version of Enlightenment rationalism, spiced with an anticlerical animus that seems an inevitable response to the reactionary-clerical atmosphere of eighteenth-century Bavaria. A somewhat naive and utopian movement which aspired ultimately to bring the human race under the rules of reason, it made many converts after 1780 among outstanding dukes and princes of the German states, and is reported to have had the allegiance of such men as Herder, Goethe, and Pestalozzi. Although the order of the Illuminati was shattered by persecution in its native principality, its humanitarian rationalism appears to have acquired a fairly wide influence in Masonic lodges. It is very easy to believe that it was attractive to some radicals with a conspiratorial cast of mind.

Americans first learned of Illuminism in 1797, from a volume published in Edinburgh (later reprinted in New York) under the title *Proofs of a Conspiracy Against All the Religions and Governments of Europe, carried on in the Secret Meetings of Free Masons, Illuminati, and Reading Societies.* Its author was a well-known Scottish scientist, John Robison, who had himself been a somewhat casual adherent of Masonry in Britain, but whose imagination had been inflamed by what he considered to be the far less innocent Masonic movement on the Continent. Robison's book was a conscientious account, laboriously pieced together out of the German sources, of the origins and development of Weishaupt's movement. For the most part, Robison seems to have made his work as factual as he could, but when he came to estimating the moral character and the political influence of Illuminism, he made the characteristic paranoid leap into fantasy. The association, he thought, was formed, "for the express purpose of rooting out all the religious establishments, and overturning all the existing governments of Europe." The most active leaders of the French Revolution, he claimed, were members; it had become "one great and wicked project fermenting and working all over Europe," and to it he attributed a central role in bringing about the French Revolution. He saw it as a libertine, anti-Christian movement, given to the corruption of women, the cultivation of sensual pleasures, and the violation of property rights. Its members had plans for making a tea that caused abortion, a secret substance that "blinds or kills when spurted in the face," and a device that sounds like a stench bomb—a "method for filling a bed-chamber with pestilential vapours."[4]

. . . .

These notions were quick to make themselves felt in America, even though it is uncertain whether any member of the Illuminati ever came here. In May 1798, a prominent minister of the Massachusetts Congregational establishment in Boston, Jedidiah Morse, delivered a timely sermon of great import to the young country, which was then sharply divided between Jeffersonians and Federalists, Francophiles and Anglophiles. After reading Robison, Morse was convinced that the United States too was the victim of a Jacobinical plot touched off by Illuminism, and that the country should be rallied to defend itself against the machinations of the international conspiracy. His warnings· were heeded throughout New England wherever Federalists brooded about the rising tide of religious infidelity or Jeffersonian democracy. Timothy Dwight, the president of Yale, followed Morse's sermon with a Fourth of July discourse, *The Duty of Americans in the Present Crisis*, in which he held forth against the Antichrist in his own glowing rhetoric.

. . . .

. . . Soon the pulpits of New England were ringing with denunciations of the Illuminati, as though the country were swarming with them.

. . . .

The anti-Masonic movement of the late 1820's and 1830's took up and extended the obsession with conspiracy. At first blush, this movement may seem to be no more than an extension or repetition of the anti-Masonic theme sounded in the earlier outcry against the Bavarian Illuminati—and, indeed, the works of writers like Robison and Barruel were often cited again as evidence of the sinister character of Masonry.

---

[4] Robison: *Proofs of a Conspiracy* (New York: 1798), pp. 14, 376, 311. For a detailed study of the American response to Illuminism, see Vernon Stauffer: *New England and the Bavarian Illuminati* (New York: 1918).

But whereas the panic of the 1790's was confined mainly to New England and linked to an ultra-conservative argument, the later anti-Masonic movement affected many parts of the northern United States and was altogether congenial to popular democracy and rural egalitarianism. Although anti-Masonry happened to be anti-Jacksonian (Jackson was a Mason), it showed the same fear that opportunists for the common man would be closed, the same passionate dislike of aristocratic institutions that one finds in the Jacksonian crusade against the Bank of the United States.

The anti-Masonic movement, though a product of spontaneous enthusiasm, soon fell victim to the changing fortunes of party politics. It was joined and used by a great many men who did not share its original anti-Masonic feelings. It attracted, for example, the support of several reputable statesmen who had only mild sympathy with its fundamental bias, but who as politicians could not afford to ignore it. Still, it was a folk movement of considerable power, and the rural enthusiasts who provided its real impetus believed in it wholeheartedly.

. . . .

Since Masons were pledged to come to each other's aid under circumstances of distress, and to extend fraternal indulgence at all times, it was held that the order nullified the enforcement of regular law. Masonic constables, sheriffs, juries, judges, and the like would all be in league with Masonic criminals and fugitives. The press too was held to have been so "muzzled" by Masonic editors and proprietors that news of Masonic malfeasance could be suppressed—which was the main reason why so shocking a scandal as the Morgan case had received relatively little publicity. Finally, at a moment when practically every alleged citadel of privilege in America was under democratic assault, Masonry was held to be a fraternity of the privileged classes, closing business opportunities and nearly monopolizing political offices, thus shutting out hardy common citizens of the type the anti-Masonic movement liked to claim for its own.

There may have been certain elements of truth and reality in these views of Masonry, and many distinguished and responsible leaders accepted them, at least in part. Not all of these charges and fears need be dismissed as entirely without foundation. What must be emphasized here, however, is the apocalyptic and absolutist framework in which this hostility to Masonry was usually expressed. Anti-Masons were not content simply to say that secret societies were rather a bad idea. David Bernard, in the standard handbook of anti-Masonic materials, *Light on Masonry*, declared that Freemasonry was the most dangerous institution that ever was imposed on man, "an engine of Satan . . . dark, unfruitful, selfish, demoralizing, blasphemous, murderous, anti-republican and anti-Christian."[5] One of the many anti-Masonic pulpit orators called the order "a work of darkness because it bears decided marks of being one of the confederate powers of iniquity predicted by the apostle John . . . which would combine the world in arms against God, and be overcome at the battle of the great day just before the millennium."[6]

. . . .

III

Fear of a Masonic plot had hardly been quieted when rumors arose of a Catholic plot against American values. One finds here again the same frame of mind, the same conviction of a conspiracy against a way of life, but now a different villain. Of course, the anti-Catholic movement converged with a growing nativism, and while they were not identical, together they cut such a wide swath in American life that they were bound to embrace many moderates to whom the paranoid style, in its full glory, did not appeal. Moreover, we need not dismiss out of hand as wholly parochial or mean-spirited the desire of Yankee Americans to maintain an ethnically and religiously homogeneous society, nor the particular Protestant commitments to individualism and freedom that were brought into play. But the movement had a large paranoid infusion, and the most influential anti-Catholic militants certainly had a strong affinity for the paranoid style.

Two books which appeared in 1835 described the new danger to the American way of life, and may be taken as expressions of the anti-Catholic mentality. One, *Foreign Conspiracy against the Liberties of the United States*, was from the hand of the celebrated painter and inventor of the telegraph, S.F.B. Morse, who was the son of Jedidiah Morse, the anti-Illuminist. "A conspiracy exists," Morse proclaimed, and "its plans are already in operation . . . we are attacked in a vulnerable quarter which cannot be defended by our ships, our forts, or our armies." In the great war going on in the Western world between political reaction and

---

[5] *Light on Masonry* (Utica: 1829), pp. iii, x. *The Address of the United States Anti-Masonic Convention* (Philadelphia: 1830) asserted (p. 17): "The abuses of which we complain involve the highest crimes of which man can be guilty, because they indicate the deepest malice, and the most fatal aim. They bespeak the most imminent danger, because they have proceeded from a conspiracy more numerous and better organized for mischief, than any other detailed in the records of man, and yet, though exposed, maintaining itself, in all its monstrous power."

[6] Griffin, *op. cit.*, pp. 27–80.

ultramontanism on one side and political and religious liberties on the other, America was a bastion of freedom, and hence an inevitable target for popes and despots. The main source of the conspiracy Morse found in Metternich's government: *"Austria is now acting in this country.* She has devised a grand scheme. She has organized a great plan for doing something here. . . . She has her Jesuit missionaries travelling through the land; she has supplied them with money, and has furnished a fountain for a regular supply."[7]

"It is an ascertained fact," wrote another Protestant militant,

> that Jesuits are prowling about all parts of the United States in every possible disguise, expressly to ascertain the advantageous situations and modes to disseminate Popery. A minister of the Gospel from Ohio has informed us that he discovered one carrying on his devices in his congregation; and he says that the western country swarms with them under the names of puppet show men, dancing masters, music teachers, peddlers of images and ornaments, barrel organ players, and similar practitioners.[8]

. . . .

Lyman Beecher, the elder of a famous family and the father of Harriet Beecher Stowe, wrote in the same year his *Plea for the West,* in which he considered the possibility that the Christian millennium might come in the American states. Everything depended, in his judgment, upon what influences dominated the great West, where the future of the country lay. There Protestantism was engaged in a life-or-death struggle with Catholicism. Time was already running out. "Whatever we do, it must be done quickly. . . . " A great tide of immigration, hostile to free institutions, was sweeping in upon the country, subsidized and sent by "the potentates of Europe," multiplying tumult and violence, filling jails, crowding poorhouses, quadrupling taxation, and sending increasing thousands of voters to "lay their inexperienced hand upon the helm of our power." Well might we believe, said Beecher, that Metternich knew that there would be a party in the United States willing to hasten the naturalization and enfranchisement of these multitudes and demagogues, a party that would "sell their country into an everlasting bondage." Even so much as a tenth of the voting population, "condensed and wielded by the Catholic powers of Europe, might decide our elections, perplex our policy, inflame and divide the nation, break the bond of our union, and throw down our free institutions."[9] Beecher did not approve violations of the civil rights of Cath-

---

[7] Morse: *Foreign Conspiracy . . .* (New York: 1835), pp. 14, 21.
[8] Quoted in Ray Allen Billington: *The Protestant Crusade* (New York: 1938), p. 120.
[9] Lyman Beecher: *Plea for the West* (Cincinnati: 1835), pp. 47, 62–3.

olics or the burning of convents, but he urged Protestants to a greater militancy and solidarity to fend off a fate that might be waiting for them in a not very distant future.

Anti-Catholicism has always been the pornography of the Puritan. Whereas the anti-Masons had imagined wild drinking bouts and had entertained themselves with fantasies about the actual enforcement of grisly Masonic oaths, the anti-Catholics developed an immense lore about libertine priests, the confessional as an opportunity for seduction, licentious convents and monasteries, and the like. Probably the most widely read contemporary book in the United States before *Uncle Tom's Cabin* was a work supposedly written by one Maria Monk, entitled *Awful Disclosures*, which appeared in 1836. The author, who purported to have escaped from the Hotel Dieu nunnery in Montreal after a residence of five years as novice and nun, reported her convent life there in elaborate and circumstantial detail. She recalled having been told by the Mother Superior that she must "obey the priests in all things"; to her "utter astonishment and horror," she soon found what the nature of such obedience was. Infants born of convent liaisons were baptized and then killed, she said, so that they might ascend at once to heaven. A high point in the *Awful Disclosures* was Maria Monk's eyewitness account of the strangling of two babies. Her book, hotly attacked and as hotly defended, continued to be read and believed even after her mother, a Protestant living near Montreal, gave testimony that Maria had been somewhat addled ever since childhood when she had rammed a pencil into her head. It was, indeed, read and believed by a dwindling audience even when poor Maria produced a fatherless child two years after the appearance of her book. She died in prison in 1849, after having been arrested in a brothel as a pickpocket.[10]

Anti-Catholicism, like anti-Masonry, mixed its fortunes with American party politics. To trace its political career would take us too far afield, but it did become an enduring factor in American politics. The American Protective Association of the 1890's revived it with ideological variations more suitable to the times—the depression of 1893, for example, was alleged to be an intentional creation of the Catholics, who began it by starting a run on the banks. Some spokesmen of the movement circulated a bogus encyclical attributed to Leo XIII instructing American Catholics on a certain date in 1893 to exterminate all

---

[10] Maria Monk: *Awful Disclosures* (New York: 1836; facsimile ed., Hamden, Conn.. 1962); see R. A. Billington's introduction to the 1962 edition and his account in *The Protestant Crusade*, pp. 99-108.

heretics, and a great many anti-Catholics daily expected a nation-wide uprising. The myth of an impending Catholic war of mutilation and extermination of heretics persisted into the twentieth century.[11]

IV

If we now take the long jump to the contemporary right wing, we find some rather important differences from the nineteenth-century movements. The spokesman of those earlier movements felt that they stood for causes and personal types that were still in possession of their country—that they were fending off threats to a still well-established way of life in which they played an important part. But the modern right wing, as Daniel Bell has put it,[12] feels dispossessed: America has been largely taken away from them and their kind, though they are determined to try to repossess it and to prevent the final destructive act of subversion. The old American virtues have already been eaten away by cosmopolitans and intellectuals; the old competitive capitalism has been gradually undermined by socialist and communist schemers; the old national security and independence have been destroyed by treasonous plots, having as their most powerful agents not merely outsiders and foreigners but major statesmen seated at the very centers of American power. Their predecessors discovered foreign conspiracies; the modern radical right finds that conspiracy also embraces betrayal at home.

Important changes may be traced to the effects of the mass media. The villains of the modern right are much more vivid than those of their paranoid predecessors, much better known to the public; the contemporary literature of the paranoid style is by the same token richer and more circumstantial in personal description and personal invective. For the vaguely delineated villains of the anti-Masons, for the obscure and disguised Jesuit agents, the little-known papal delegates of the anti-Catholics, for the shadowy international bankers of the monetary

---

[11] John Higham: *Strangers in the Land* (New Brunswick, N.J.: 1955), pp. 81, 85, 180. Higham, studying Henry F. Bowers, a leader of this later phase of anti-Catholicism, finds "a mind charged with constant excitement and given to rigid categorical judgments," moving "in a world of suspicion and imagined danger. Here a single hostile force explained the trivial events of daily experience, while a sense of grandeur and destiny sustained the struggle against it. Everywhere Bowers saw evidence of the machinations of a foreign ecclesiastical conspiracy endowed with immense power." "The Mind of a Nativist: Henry F. Bowers and the A.P.A.," *American Quarterly*, IV (Spring, 1953), 21.

[12] "The Dispossessed," in Daniel Bell (ed.): *The Radical Right* (New York: 1963), pp. 1–38.

conspiracies, we may now substitute eminent public figures like Presidents Roosevelt, Truman, and Eisenhower, Secretaries of State like Marshall, Acheson, and Dulles, justices of the Supreme Court like Frankfurter and Warren, and the whole battery of lesser but still famous and vivid conspirators headed by Alger Hiss.[13]

Events since 1939 have given the contemporary right-wing paranoid a vast theater for his imagination, full of rich and proliferating detail, replete with realistic clues and undeniable proofs of the validity of his views. The theater of action is now the entire world, and he can draw on not only the events of the Second World War but those of the Korean War and the cold war. Any historian of warfare knows that it is in good part a comedy of errors and a museum of incompetence; but if for every error and every act of incompetence one can substitute an act of treason, we can see how many points of fascinating interpretation are open to the paranoid imagination: treason in high places can be found at almost every turning—and in the end the real mystery, for one who reads the primary works of paranoid scholarship, is not how the United States has been brought to its present dangerous position, but how it has managed to survive at all.

The basic elements of contemporary right-wing thought can be reduced to three: First, there has been the now familiar sustained conspiracy, running over more than a generation, and reaching its climax in Roosevelt's New Deal, to undermine free capitalism, to bring the economy under the direction of the federal government, and to pave the way for socialism or communism. Details might be open to argument among right-wingers, but many would agree with Frank Chodorov, the author of, The Income Tax: The Root of All Evil,[14] that this

[13] The appeal of the conspiratorial conception of power is brilliantly and economically set against its historical background by Edward Shils: The Torment of Secrecy (Glencoe, Ill.: 1956), esp. Ch. I.

[14] New York, 1954, esp. Ch. 5. For a good brief summary of the history of this alleged conspiracy, see Chesly Manly: The Twenty-Year Revolution: From Roosevelt to Eisenhower (Chicago: 1954), which traces all aspects of the "revolution" and finds in the United Nations (p. 179) "the principal instrument of a gigantic conspiracy to control the foreign and domestic policies of the United States, subvert the Constitution, and establish a totalitarian society." A more recent and much more widely read work, particularly popular in the Goldwater movement, is Phyllis Schlafly's A Choice Not an Echo. (Alton, Ill.: 1964), which traces the work of a small group of "secret kingmakers" in New York who have controlled the affairs of the Republican party from 1936 to 1960. . . . A more substantial contemporary manual of conspiratorial views, which traces ramifications in many areas of American life, is John A. Stormer: None Dare Call It Treason (Florissant, Mo.: 1964).

campaign began with the passage of the income tax amendment to the Constitution in 1913.

The second contention is that top government officialdom has been so infiltrated by Communists that American policy, at least since the days leading up to Pearl Harbor, has been dominated by sinister men who were shrewdly and consistently selling out American national interests.

The final contention is that the country is infused with a network of Communist agents, just as in the old days it was infiltrated by Jesuit agents, so that the whole apparatus of education, religion, the press, and the mass media are engaged in a common effort to paralyze the resistance of loyal Americans.

The details of the modern right-wing case are beyond the scope of any brief discussion. Perhaps the most representative document of its McCarthyist phase was a long indictment of Secretary of State George C. Marshall, delivered in the Senate on June 14, 1951, by Senator Mc-Carthy, and later published in a somewhat different form as *America's Retreat from Victory: The Story of George Catlett Marshall.* McCarthy pictured Marshall as the focal figure in a betrayal of American interests stretching in time from the strategic plans for the Second World War to the formulation of the Marshall Plan. Marshall was associated with practically every American failure or defeat, McCarthy insisted, and none of this was due to either accident or incompetence. There was a "baffling pattern" of Marshall's interventions in the war: "His deci-sions, maintained with great stubbornness and skill, always and invariably serv[ed] the world policy of the Kremlin." Under his guidance there was conducted at the end of the war "what appeared to be a planned loss of the peace." Marshall's report on his mission to China cannot be understood as the product of incompetence, but appears persuasive and brilliant when it is read as "a propaganda document in behalf of other interests, another country and civilization." Marshall and Acheson were intent on delivering China to Russia. The Marshall Plan was "an evil hoax on the generosity, good will and carelessness of the American people." And, above all, the sharp decline in America's relative strength from 1945 to 1951 did not "just happen," it was "brought about, step by step, by will and intention," the consequence not of mistakes but of a treasonous conspiracy, "a conspiracy on a scale so immense as to dwarf any previous such venture in the history of man." The ultimate aim of this conspiracy was "that we shall be con-tained and frustrated and finally fall victim to Soviet intrigue from within and Russian military might from without."[15]

Today the mantle of McCarthy has fallen on the retired candy manufacturer Robert H. Welch, Jr., who is less strategically placed but whose well-organized following in the John Birch Society has had a strong influence. A few years ago Welch proclaimed that "Communist influences are now in almost complete control of our Federal Government"—note the care and scrupulousness of that "almost." He has offered a full-scale interpretation of our recent history in which Communists figure at every turn: They started a run on American banks in 1933 that forced their closure; they contrived the recognition of the Soviet Union by the United States in the same year, just in time to save the Soviets from economic collapse; they have stirred up the fuss over segregation; they have taken over the Supreme Court and made it "one of the most important agencies of Communism." They are winning the struggle for control in "the press, the pulpit, the radio and television media, the labor unions, the schools, the courts, and the legislative halls of America."

Close attention to history wins for Mr. Welch an insight into affairs that is given to few of us. "For many reasons and after a lot of study," he wrote some years ago, "I personally believe [John Foster] Dulles to be a Communist agent." Other apparently innocent figures are similarly unmasked. The job of Professor Arthur F. Burns as the head of Eisenhower's Council of Economic Advisers quite probably was "merely a coverup for Burns' liaison work between Eisenhower and some of his bosses in the Establishment." Eisenhower's brother Milton was "actually [his] superior and boss within the whole Leftwing Establishment." As for Eisenhower himself, Welch characterized him, in words that have made the candy manufacturer famous, as "a dedicated, conscious agent of the Communist conspiracy"—a conclusion, he added, "based on an accumulation of detailed evidence so extensive and so palpable that it seems to put this conviction beyond any reasonable doubt."[16]

. . . .

---

[15] Joseph R. McCarthy: *America's Retreat from Victory* (New York: 1951), pp. 54, 66, 130, 141, 156, 168, 169, 171.

[16] *The Politician* (Belmont, Mass.: 1963), pp. 222, 223, 229. Quotations from Welch vary slightly because his incredible diatribe against Eisenhower was modified in later editions of this book—for example, Eisenhower was later described as (p. 291) "either a willing agent, or an integral and important part of a conspiracy of gangsters determined to rule the world at any cost." Welch's views are ably summarized by Alan Westin, from a different version of the text, in "The John Birch Society," in Daniel Bell (ed): *op. cit.*, pp. 204–6.

V

. . . The paranoid spokesman sees the fate of this conspiracy in apocalyptic terms—he traffics in the birth and death of whole worlds, whole political orders, whole systems of human values. He is always manning the barricades of civilization. He constantly lives at a turning point: it is now or never in organizing resistance to conspiracy. Time is forever just running out. Like religious millenarians, he expresses the anxiety of those who are living through the last days and he is sometimes disposed to set a date for the apocalypse. "Time is running out," said Welch in 1951. "Evidence is piling up on many sides and from many sources that October 1952 is the fatal month when Stalin will attack." [17]

. . . .

As a member of the avant-garde who is capable of perceiving the conspiracy before it is fully obvious to an as yet unaroused public, the paranoid is a militant leader. He does not see social conflict as something to be mediated and compromised, in the manner of the working politician. Since what is at stake is always a conflict between absolute good and absolute evil, the quality needed is not a willingness to compromise but the will to fight things out to a finish. Nothing but complete victory will do. Since the enemy is thought of as being totally evil and totally unappeasable, he must be totally eliminated—if not from the world, at least from the theater of operations to which the paranoid directs his attention. This demand for unqualified victories leads to the formulation of hopelessly demanding and unrealistic goals, and since these goals are not even remotely attainable, failure constantly heightens the paradnoid's frustration. Even partial success leaves him with the same sense of powerlessness with which he began, and this in turn only strengthens his awareness of the vast and terrifying quality of the enemy he opposes.

This enemy is clearly delineated: he is a perfect model of malice, a kind of amoral superman: sinister, ubiquitous, powerful, cruel, sensual, luxury-loving. Unlike the rest of us, the enemy is not caught in the toils of the vast mechanism of history, himself a victim of his past, his desires, his limitations. He is a free, active, demonic agent. He wills, indeed he manufactures, the mechanism of history himself, or

---

[17] *May God Forgive Us* (Chicago: 1952), p. 73. Dr. Fred C. Schwarz of the Christian Anti-Communism Crusade is more circumspect. In his lectures he sets the year 1973 as the date for the Communists to achieve control of the world, if they are not stopped. Most contemporary paranoid spokesmen speak of a "Communist timetable," of whose focal dates they often seem to have intimate knowledge.

deflects the normal course of history in an evil way. He makes crises, starts runs on banks, causes depressions, manufactures disasters, and then enjoys and profits from the misery he has produced. The paranoid's interpretation of history is in this sense distinctly personal: decisive events are not taken as part of the stream of history, but as the consequences of someone's will. Very often the enemy is held to possess some especially effective source of power: he controls the press; he directs the public mind through "managed news"; he has unlimited funds; he has a new secret for influencing the mind (brainwashing); he has a special technique for seduction (the Catholic confessional); he is gaining a stranglehold on the educational system.

This enemy seems to be on many counts a projection of the self: both the ideal and the unacceptable aspects of the self are attributed to him. A fundamental paradox of the paranoid style is the imitation of the enemy. The enemy, for example, may be the cosmopolitan intellectual, but the paranoid will outdo him in the apparatus of scholarship, even of pedantry. Senator McCarthy, with his heavily documented tracts and his show of information, Mr. Welch with his accumulations of irresistible evidence, John Robison with his laborious study of documents in a language he but poorly used, the anti-Masons with their endlessly painstaking discussions of Masonic ritual—all these offer a kind of implicit compliment to their opponents. Secret organizations set up to combat secret organizations give the same flattery. The Ku Klux Klan imitated Catholicism to the point of donning priestly vestments, developing an elaborate ritual and an equally elaborate hierarchy. The John Birch Society emulates Communist cells and quasi-secret operation through "front" groups, and preaches a ruthless prosecution of the ideological war along lines very similar to those it finds in the Communist enemy. Spokesmen of the various Christian anti-Communist "crusades" openly express their admiration for the dedication, discipline, and strategic ingenuity the Communist cause calls forth.

. . . .

Much of the function of the enemy lies not in what can be imitated but in what can be wholly condemned. The sexual freedom often attributed to him, his lack of moral inhibition, his possession of especially effective techniques for fulfilling his desires, give exponents of the paranoid style an opportunity to project and freely express unacceptable aspects of their own minds. Priests and Mormon patriarchs were commonly thought to have especial attraction for women, and hence licentious privilege. Thus Catholics and Mormons—later Negroes and

Jews—lent themselves to a preoccupation with illicit sex. Very often the fantasies of true believers serve as strong sado-masochistic outlets, vividly expressed, for example, in the concern of anti-Masons with the alleged cruelty of Masonic punishments.

. . . .

Another recurring aspect of the paranoid style is the special significance that attaches to the figure of the renegade from the enemy cause. The anti-Masonic movement seemed at times to be the creation of ex-Masons; it certainly attached the highest significance and gave the most unqualified credulity to their revelations. Similarly anti-Catholicism used the runaway nun and the apostate priest, anti-Mormonism the ex-wife from the harem of polygamy; the avant-garde anti-Communist movements of our time use the ex-Communist. In some part the special authority accorded the renegade derives from the obsession with secrecy so characteristic of such movements: the renegade is the man or woman who has been in the secret world of the enemy, and brings forth with him or her the final verification of suspicions which might otherwise have been doubted by a skeptical world. But I think there is a deeper eschatological significance attached to the person of the renegade: in the spiritual wrestling match between good and evil which is the paranoid's archetypal model of the world struggle, the renegade is living proof that all the conversions are not made by the wrong side. He brings with him the promise of redemption and victory.

In contemporary right-wing movements a particularly important part has been played by ex-Communists who have moved rapidly, though not without anguish, from the paranoid left to the paranoid right, clinging all the while to the fundamentally Manichean psychology that underlies both. Such authorities on communism remind one of those ancient converts from paganism to Christianity of whom it is told that upon their conversion they did not entirely cease to believe in their old gods but converted them into demons.

A final aspect of the paranoid style is related to that quality of pedantry to which I have already referred. One of the impressive things about paranoid literature is precisely the elaborate concern with demonstration it almost invariably shows. One should not be misled by the fantastic conclusions that are so characteristic of this political style into imagining that it is not, so to speak, argued out along factual lines. The very fantastic character of its conclusions leads to heroic strivings for "evidence" to prove that the unbelievable is the only thing that can be believed. Of course, there are highbrow, lowbrow, and middlebrow

paranoids, as there are likely to be in any political tendency, and paranoid movements from the Middle Ages onward have had a magnetic
attraction for demi-intellectuals. But respectable paranoid literature
not only starts from certain moral commitments that can be justified
to many non-paranoids but also carefully and all but obsessively
accumulates "evidence." Paranoid writing begins with certain defensible judgments. There *was* something to be said for the anti-
Masons. After all, a secret society composed on influential men bound
by special obligations could conceivably pose some kind of threat to the
civil order in which they were suspended. There was also something to
be said for the Protestant principles of individuality and freedom, as
well as for the nativist desire to develop in North America a homog-
enous civilization. Again, in our time innumerable decisions of the
Second World War and the cold war can be faulted, and it is easy for the
suspicious to believe that such decisions are not simply the mistakes of
well-meaning men but the plans of traitors.

The typical procedure of the higher paranoid scholarship is to start
with such defensible assumptions and with a careful accumulation of
facts, or at least of what appear to be facts, and to marshal these facts
toward an overwhelming "proof" of the particular conspiracy that is
to be established. It is nothing if not coherent—in fact, the paranoid
mentality is far more coherent than the real world, since it leaves no
room for mistakes, failures, or ambiguities. It is, if not wholly rational,
at least intensely rationalistic; it believes that it is up against an enemy
who is as infallibly rational as he is totally evil, and it seeks to match
his imputed total competence with its own, leaving nothing unex-
plained and comprehending all of reality in one overreaching, consistent
theory. It is nothing if not "scholarly" in technique. McCarthy's 96-page
pamphlet *McCarthyism* contains no less than 313 footnote references,
and Mr. Welch's fantastic assault on Eisenhower, *The Politician*, is
weighed down by a hundred pages of bibliography and notes. The entire
right-wing movement of our time is a parade of experts, study groups,
monographs, footnotes, and bibliographies. Sometimes the right-wing
striving for scholarly depth and an inclusive world view has startling
consequences: Mr. Welch, for example, has charged that the popu-
larity of Arnold Toynbee's historical work is the consequence of a plot
on the part of Fabians, "Labour Party bosses in England," and various
members of the Anglo-American "liberal establishment" to over-

shadow the much more truthful and illuminating work of Oswald Spengler.[18]

. . . .

Since I have drawn so heavily on American examples, I would like to emphasize again that the paranoid style is an international phenomenon. Nor is it confined to modern times. Studying the millennial sects of Europe from the eleventh to the sixteenth century, Norman Cohn finds, in his brilliant book *The Pursuit of the Millennium,* a persistent psychological complex that closely resembles what I have been considering—a style made up of certain marked preoccupations and fantasies: "the megalomanic view of oneself as the Elect, wholly good, abominably persecuted yet assured of ultimate triumph; the attribution of gigantic and demonic powers to the adversary; the refusal to accept the ineluctable limitations and imperfections of human existence, such as transience, dissention, conflict, fallibility whether intellectual or moral; the obsession with inerrable prophecies . . . systematized misinterpretations, always gross and often grotesque . . . ruthlessness directed towards an end which by its very nature cannot be realised—towards a total and final solution such as cannot be attained at any actual time or in any concrete situation, but only in the timeless and autistic realm of phantasy."[19]

The recurrence of the paranoid style over a long span of time and in different places suggests that a mentality disposed to see the world in the paranoid's way may always be present in some considerable minority of the population. But the fact that movements employing the paranoid style are not constant but come in successive episodic waves suggests that the paranoid disposition is mobilized into action chiefly by social conflicts that involve ultimate schemes of values and that bring fundamental fears and hatreds, rather than negotiable interests, into political action. Catastrophe or the fear of catastrophe is most likely to elicit the syndrome of paranoid rhetoric.

[18] *The Blue Book of the John Birch Society* (Belmont, Mass.: J.B.S., 1961), pp. 42–3.

[19] *The Pursuit of the Millennium* (London: 1957), pp. 309–10; see also pp. 58–75. In the Middle Ages millenarianism flourished among the poor, the oppressed, and the hopeless. In Anglo-American experience, as Samuel Shepperson has observed, such movements have never been confined to these classes, but have had a more solid middle-class foundation. "The Comparative Study of Millenarian Movements," in Sylvia Thrupp (ed.): *Millennial Dreams in Action* (The Hague: 1962), pp. 49–52.

In American experience, ethnic and religious conflicts, with their threat of the submergence of whole systems of values, have plainly been the major focus for militant and suspicious minds of this sort, but elsewhere class conflicts have also mobilized such energies. The paranoid tendency is aroused by a confrontation of opposed interests which are (or are felt to be) totally irreconcilable, and thus by nature not susceptible to the normal political processes of bargain and compromise. The situation becomes worse when the representatives of a particular political interest—perhaps because of the very unrealistic and unrealizable nature of their demands—cannot make themselves felt in the political process. Feeling that they have no access to political bargaining or the making of decisions, they find their original conception of the world of power as omnipotent, sinister, and malicious fully confirmed. They see only the consequences of power—and this through distorting lenses—and have little chance to observe its actual machinery. L. B. Namier once said that "the crowning attainment of historical study" is to achieve "an intuitive sense of how things do not happen."[20] It is precisely this kind of awareness that the paranoid fails to develop. He has a special resistance of his own, of course, to such awareness, but circumstances often deprive him of exposure to events that might enlighten him. We are all sufferers from history, but the paranoid is a double sufferer, since he is afflicted not only by the real world, with the rest of us, but by his fantasies as well.

---

[20] L. B. Namier: "History," in Fritz Stern (ed.): *The Varieties of History* (New York: 1956), p. 375.

Suggestions for Further Reading

The student interested in furthering his knowledge of the extreme right could do no better than to start with Daniel Bell, ed., *The Radical Right* (New York: Doubleday-Anchor, 1963). Here a distinguished group of social scientists, including Bell, Richard Hofstadter, David Riesman, Nathan Glazer, Peter Viereck and Talcott Parsons, among others, approach the problem from the points of view of various disciplines and achieve a number of penetrating insights into the phenomenon of extremism. The collection is especially interesting because it contains essays both from the mid-fifties and the early sixties, thus giving an idea of the shifting perspectives on the rightists.

Less important than Bell's collection, but of use to anyone who wants an introduction to the wide scope of extreme right activities, are a number of more-or-less journalistic accounts that have appeared in book form. All of these share the same virtues and defects; each has a wealth of information and anecdotal detail about rightist organizations, yet all are short on analysis of these groups. Indeed, their analysis usually consists of insights taken from the essays in the Bell collection. Still, each of the works is helpful in shedding light on this topic.

This group includes the following: Brooks R. Walker, *The Christian Fright Peddlers* (New York: Doubleday, 1964); Donald Janson and Bernard Eismann, *The Far Right* (New York: McGraw-Hill, 1963); Mark Sherwin, *The Extremists* (New York: St. Martin's, 1963); Harry and Bonaro Overstreet, *The Strange Tactics of Extremism* (New York: Norton, 1964); and Arnold Forster and Benjamin R. Epstein, *Danger on the Right* (New York: Random House, 1964). One book which deals in part with the topic is Edward Cain, *They'd Rather Be Right* (New York: Macmillan, 1963), a portrait of youth and various conservative movements. Roger Burlingame, *The Sixth Column* (Philadelphia: Lippincott, 1962), which traces rightist groups from the First World War to 1960, puts extremism in historical perspective.

Magazines have had a field day writing about extremism; any comprehensive list of their work would be very long. Here only a few samples will be mentioned. Surveys of the right include Alan Barth, "Report on the Rampageous Right," *New York Times Magazine* (Nov. 26, 1961); Arthur M. Schlesinger, Jr., "The Threat of the Radical Right," *New York Times Magazine* (June 17, 1962); and Fred J. Cook, "The Ultras," *Nation* (June 30, 1962). A look at Billy James Hargis can be found in H. H. Martin, "Doomsday Merchant on the Far, Far Right," *Saturday Evening Post* (April 28, 1962), while the effect of extremism on the churches is considered in Howard and Arlene Eisenberg, "The Far Right and the Churches," *Progressive* (July and August, 1965). A humorous portrait of the New England Rally for God, Family and Country is painted in Judith Rascoe, "For Garden Country: Rally on the Right," *Atlantic* (September, 1966). Attacks by rightists on the PTA are described in E. Dunbar, "Plot to Take Over the PTA," *Look* (September 7, 1965), and attempts of the John Birch Society to spy on professors at the University of Texas are revealed in Willie Morris, "Cell 772, or Life Among the Extremists," *Commentary* (October, 1964).

For the most part, the preceding articles are descriptive. The student interested in deeper analyses of extremism must go to various scholarly publications, where social scientists have been reporting their findings on the subject. *The Journal of Social Issues*, XIX (April, 1963), is devoted entirely to "American Political Extremism in the 1960's." Included are half a dozen articles, among them being "Responsible and Irresponsible Right-Wing Groups: A Problem in Analysis," "Participant Observation in a Super-Patriot Discussion Group," and "On Super-Patriotism: A Definition and Analysis." The last of these is an attempt to define extremism precisely; another such attempt can be found in G. B. Rush, "Toward a Definition of the Extreme Right," *The Pacific Sociological Review*, VI (Fall, 1963).

The intellectual background of the right is probed in Victor C. Ferkiss, "Political and Intellectual Origins of the American Radical, Right and Left," *The Annals*, CCCXLIV (November, 1962), while Arnold Forster, "Violence on the Fanatical Left and Right," *The Annals*, CCCLXIV (March, 1966), considers the idea that extremism will result in violence. Various articles take up the problem of what causes extremism. Alienation as a cause is considered in Gilbert Abcarian and Sherman M. Stanage, "Alienation and the Radical Right," *Journal of Politics*, XXVII (November, 1965). Everett C. Ladd, Jr., "The Radical Right: White Collar Extremists," *South Atlantic Quarterly*, LXV (Summer, 1966), thinks the phenomenon is primarily due to the expansion of the middle class since World War II. The role of the Catholic in far right movements is explored in Edward T. Gargan, "Radical Catholics of the Right," *Social Order* (November, 1961) and Stanley Rothman, "American Catholics and the Radical Right," *Social Order* (April, 1963).

One of the most interesting discussions is Raymond Wolfinger et al., "America's Radical Right: Politics and Ideology," in David Apter, ed., *Ideology and Discontent* (New York: Free Press, 1964). This is a study of people who attended a Christian Anti-Communism Crusade School in Oakland, California; in analyzing their social and ideological backgrounds, the authors manage to call into question many conclusions reached by other students of the right. Finally, D. K. Stewart and T. C. Smith, "Celebrity Structure of the Far Right," *Western Political Quarterly*, XVII (June, 1964) gives an insight into the overlapping leadership of rightist organizations.

Most interest in extremism has centered around the John Birch Society, and much has been written about it. Thomas M. Storke, "How Some Birchers Were Birched," *New York Times Magazine* (Dec. 10, 1961) gives an interesting account of Santa Barbara, California's encounter with the John Birch Society. Worthwhile longer studies include J. Allen Broyles, *The John Birch Society: Anatomy of a Protest* (Boston: Beacon, 1964) and Benjamin R. Epstein and Arnold Forster, *Report on The John Birch Society, 1966* (New York: Random House, 1966).